250

AMAZING FISHING TIPS

THE BEST TACTICS AND TECHNIQUES
TO CATCH ANY AND ALL GAME FISH

BASS • TROUT • PANFISH
AND MORE!

EDITED BY
LAMAR UNDERWOOD

ILLUSTRATED BY
JOHN RICE

Skyhorse Publishing

Skyhorse Publishing books may be purchased in bulk at special discounts for sales promotion, corporate gifts, fund-raising, or educational purposes. Special editions can also be created to specifications. For details, contact the Special Sales Department, Skyhorse Publishing, 307 West 36th Street, 11th Floor, New York, NY 10018 or info@skyhorsepublishing.com.

Skyhorse® and Skyhorse Publishing® are registered trademarks of Skyhorse Publishing, Inc.®, a Delaware corporation.

Visit our website at www.skyhorsepublishing.com.

10 9 8 7 6 5 4 3 2 1

Library of Congress Cataloging-in-Publication Data is available on file.

ISBN: 978-1-63220-302-1
Ebook ISBN: 978-1-63220-949-8

Printed in the United States of America

250
AMAZING FISHING TIPS

Contents

TROUT & SALMON 73

WALLEYE 103

PANFISH, CATFISH & CARP 107

PICKEREL, PIKE & MUSKIE   121

SALTWATER FISH   125

WILDERNESS FISHING   141

ICE FISHING   153

Introduction

Somewhere along the way, "tips" have left many folks with a bad taste in their mouths. They have been burned by tips, ending up buying the wrong stocks and mutual funds; seeing the wrong doctors and dentists; driving the "garage queen" SUVs; and spending their hard-earned vacations at Destination Disaster. That's to say nothing of heeding the tom-toms and chants urging them to buy products they don't really need or that don't really work.

Fishing tips are different. They are always out there, and, it would seem, we're pretty much always ready to lend an ear and hear the latest on the creek where the trout are as long as your leg; the lure so deadly you have to tie it on while hiding it from the murderous eyes of nearby fish, least risk a collision with the hurtling body of a prowling bass; the knot so strong you could tow the Queen Mary with it; and the deft retrieving motion that turns a tiny topwater lure into a creeping, crawling, wounded tidbit no predator can resist.

You might say, with considerable bite and accuracy, that this editor has had his proper turn at bat as a tip-provider. As a former editor-in-chief of both *Sports Afield* and *Outdoor Life*, in addition to other publications, and as a writer of both magazine articles and books on fishing, with the help of my collaborating publishers I have sent countless numbers of tips, dancing and singing and begging to be taken, under noses of readers. Some of them must have gotten a few strikes, or I would have been fired. Editors do not remain editors very long when their products are ignored.

Despite their sometimes tawdry reputations, fishing tips keep coming along with enough promises to attract the attention of anglers—while at the same time allowing editors to keep their jobs. This particular fusillade of tips, however, has been unleashed by this editor neither to test the strength of the marketplace nor to provide temporary employment. My goal is much more selfish, a deep personal desire to get more fun out of my fishing by spreading the word on ways to be successful.

There is a great quote from the legendary naturalist and nature-story writer Ernest Thompson Seton. One of his characters says, "Because I have known the agonies of thirst, I would dig a well so that others might drink." While not catching fish cannot be reasonably compared to the "agonies of thirst," the state of mind where one reaches out to others with a helping hand has rewarded generations of anglers. And now that I find myself fishing the "Seniors Creek," I have discovered, along with multitudes of my limping, gray-haired colleagues, that one can enjoy the catches and fishing pleasures of other anglers with all the joy and fervor of one's own—even more-so when you're in the boat or on the stream with a partner and see their smiles produced by trying one of your tricks or suggestions.

So confident am I of the tips presented in this book that I can anticipate the smiles and joy they are going to bring. Not every one of them will work; I know that. But so many of them will bring new fun to your fishing that I am already enjoying the idea of your success. I wish we could be in a boat or on a stream together when you try them. That not being possible, I present the best tricks, tackle, destinations, and information sources I have found that will help you catch more fish. Some of them, I can honestly say, will change the way you fish forever.

Sometimes the tip I have for you will be a certain lure, other times ways to fish certain lures. There will be tips on rewarding websites and tips on destinations. You'll find tips on every knot you need, plus ways to get help tying them. There are all kinds of tips about the habits of gamefish, and even lots of useful tips on the habits of your fellow anglers that will enable you to outfish them.

—Lamar Underwood

CHAPTER 1

Before You Go . . .

1

1. Rivers vs. Reservoirs

Reservoirs are big and perplexing. Somewhere near 90 percent of the reservoir water will have no fish. Did you get that? I repeat: *Somewhere near 90 percent of the water will have no fish.* Where are the magic spots making up the other 10 percent? Tough question. You need charts, local knowledge, and a lot of exploring on your own. Rivers are easy to read, since the fish will be lying mostly along the banks, or by rocks and logs breaking the mid-stream flow. In reservoirs, you'll need a good boat, trolling motor, and lots of electronic gear. In rivers, a canoe or johnboat will work, as will a float tube. You can also wade in certain spots. In some rivers, you'll need a trolling motor to help with positioning. In rivers you'll have to be able to get up- or downstream, or have someone drop you off and meet you at a designated spot. In reservoirs, you can launch and go fishing and come back to your vehicle anytime you want.

2. Old Impoundments Mean Tougher Fishing

The older the impoundment you're fishing, the more likely you are to get skunked or catch very few bass . . . unless you know the bottom very well. As the bass have grown larger, they have gathered into schools, and, as A.D. Livingston, *Fishing for Bass: Modern Tactics and Tackle*, (1974), says: "They have selected their feeding areas and have established migration routes. Blind trolling and random casting become less productive." Livingston says you may catch a few small bass around the shoreline cover or stickups in the lake, but unless your depth finder, charts, or the local "experts" have put you on the spots where the fish are, you're in for slim pickings.

3. Farm Pond Fishing 101

Farm ponds, of which there are millions, are great places to catch bass and panfish. Be aware, however, that many of them are virtually fished-out because of the overpopulation of runt bluegills.

As the populations of tiny bluegills increase, the bass spawn decreases. Bass are still there, however, and they can be caught. Look for them in holes or on structures where they have cover and can ambush the bluegill prey when hungry. When you find a farm pond with the bass and bluegill populations in balance, rejoice and enjoy. You'll catch big bluegills perfect for the pan and lots of battling bass.

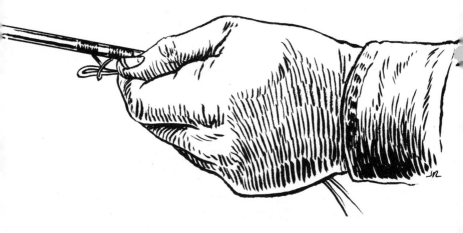

4. Stringing Up Your Fly Rod

If ever there was a "fool's errand," it's the act of trying to thread your leader and line through the guides of your fly rod by pushing the point of the leader through the ferrules first. It's like threading a needle. Instead, grasp the end of the fly line, where it's tied to the leader, and the leader itself with your thumb and forefinger and then thread the bow of leader/line through the ferrules. You'll be fishing a lot sooner.

5. Carrying Your Rod: Tip First or Butt First?

When carrying your rigged-up rod from one fishing hole to another, sometimes through brushy and rocky terrain, is it best to hold the rod tip first or butt first? The question deserves thought and debate. Tip first catches more snags and brush, and the tip is exposed to being rammed into the ground or a tree during a lax moment. Butt first seems to avoid more snags, but if you have companions coming up behind you, they may walk right into your tip. My preference, butt first, stems from seeing too many tips broken on the ground or obstructions in front of the angler.

6. Fly Reels: Direct Drive or Anti-Reverse?

Once you get the hang of fly fishing, you'll enjoy casting, fishing, and playing fish much more if you have a direct drive reel. Heavier, more-complex anti-reverse reels help novices who are inexperienced in playing fish, but they have a lot less "feel" and seem strange when you're reeling like mad and the spool's not turning (or is even going backward) because it's locked on a drag setting that's too soft for the fish you're playing. I don't think you'll ever regret going with a direct drive reel.

7. Fish Superlines Where Pickerel and Pike Roam

Even though bass or walleyes may be your target, when you're fishing waters where pickerel and pike roam, your line may meet sharp teeth. When that happens, say good-bye to your expensive lure. When I'm fishing for bass in waters that hold pike and pickerel, I've had good luck using Berkley's Fireline. There are other choices of superlines out there, of course. Some anglers do not like the feel or casting characteristics of the superlines, but I'm not in that group.

8. Frayed Superlines Won't Last

Even though superlines are very strong and resist breaking or being cut by toothy fish, they are not indestructible. If the line becomes frayed, perhaps on a snag or rock, it's going to fail at a critical moment—like when a big pike has hit your expensive swimbait.

9. More on Those Braided Superlines

The braided superlines such as FireLine, SpiderWire, and Tuf-Line, and others are getting a lot of attention from anglers these days. My experience with FireLine and SpiderWire has convinced me they are strong as all get-out and will not stretch. I like them. They are so strong that when you hang on the bottom or something, they are hard to break free. Some Internet reports I've seen have warned that these lines can cut you if handled the wrong way, bare-handed. Sometimes there are complaints of the line biting down into the line spooled on the reel. There are also caveats about which knots to use with braided lines. [See the "Knots" chapter.]

10. Rule for Fighting Big Fish

"When he pulls, you don't. When he doesn't, you do."
—Jerome B. Robinson, *Field & Stream*, March 1992

11. Casting Practice: The Absolute Necessary Evil

All athletes, from stickball to the pros, know they have to practice to master the skills they need. Why is it that so many anglers refuse to spend a little time outside practicing their casting skills? If lack of casting practice is an issue for you, consider fixing the problem and actually trying to enjoy your practice. Your fishing fun will soar as your casting improves.

12. World-Record Bass Mania

As of this writing, the world-record largemouth bass dates back to June 2, 1932, when a twenty-two-year-old Georgia farm boy named George Perry landed a 22-pound 4-ounce monster from a spot called Montgomery Lake, which may have been part of an oxbow bend of the Ocmulgee River. The fish was weighed and certified in the *Field & Stream* records caretaking of that time. The lure said to have been used was a "Creek Chub," but the exact model of the Creek Chub has been lost in controversy and lost records over the years. Today, thousands of anglers passionately fish to break Perry's record, especially in California where transplants of the Florida bass grow to prodigious sizes. Many of these anglers believe that they really have a chance to catch such a bass, and that doing so will make them wealthy. Just like buying a lottery ticket!

13. Fishing Those Golden Autumn Days

When the weather is clear and gorgeous in autumn, expect trout to be even spookier than usual—especially where the fish are running into the river from a lake or reservoir. The autumn days that bring the best fishing are *not* the calendar type. You want cloudy, rainy conditions for ripping streamers.

14. Long-Handled Nets for Shoreline Fishing

British anglers, who love shoreline fishing for all sorts of species, learned long ago that it's easier to land a fish from shore with a long-handled net that can reach out and do the job. Many are available at shops like www.cabelas.com, www.bassprshops.com, and others.

15. Florida's Winter Fishing: Cold Front Woes

You're not alone in wanting to go to Florida during the winter to get into warm weather and good fishing. And it can be done, if you're lucky. However, when cold fronts move into Florida during the winter months, the fishing shuts down just as tight as your ice-bound lake back home in Michigan. Cold fronts, particularly the extreme versions, and Florida fishing do not mix.

16. When Guides Give You a Bonus

The money you invest in a day's fishing with a good guide isn't just paying for the trip to his favorite hotspots. If he's any good, he *knows* stuff, lots of stuff. Watch him and learn his techniques. Ask questions. Consider him your professor for the kind of fishing you're doing.

17. Rods Belong in the Bag

Avoid the bugaboo of long fishing rod cases requiring special handling in the airport baggage area by using three-piece spinning rods and four-piece fly rods. They will fit into your duffle bag or other bags, and today's models cast superbly. The experience of waiting for your long rod case to emerge from the little door behind the baggage belts is not fun. The caveat is that many expert anglers, including Stu Apte, consider three-piece fly rods to be much better casters than four-piece rods. Unfortunately, three-piece rod tubes won't fit into a regular-size duffle bag.

18. When a Light Rod Is the Right Rod

Light rods that come alive in your hand, practically trembling with feeling while both working a lure or fly or fighting a fish, are irresistible. But whether fly fishing, spinning, or baitcasting is your game, one must remember that rod tip strength and lifting power are essential to good casting and fish fighting. Rods with tips that are too limp or whippy won't give you the quickness and strength you need to pop a good cast or set a hook. Repeat: You will regret ignoring tip quickness and power in all types of casting and fishing. Other than specialized situations, "slow tip" rods are not the way to go in my opinion. And remember, I'm not a casting champion, I'm just a guy trying to get a lure or fly out there, set the hook, and play the fish.

19. Polaroid Glasses: The Absolute Essential

No matter what kind of fishing you do, you shouldn't be out there without polarized glasses. Not only will they protect your eyes from any errant hooks, but they will cut the glare so you can see what's happening in the water. You can buy economy models that cost $20 to $50. With some of these, you may feel as if you need two pair, one with dark lenses for bright days and one with the lighter lenses for dull days. Personally, I like the more expensive models with copper photochromatic lenses. They adjust to any light all day long. The really good ones.

20. The Ding That Breaks a Rod

When a graphite fly rod breaks unexpectedly, say during a routine cast or while playing a small fish, the cause is often a cast that went wrong sometime before. It happened when a fly or lure dinged the rod on a Backcast or Forward Cast. Graphite can take a lot of stress and bending, but it hates dings.

21. Fly Fishing Without Casting

If you're just dying to get on the water and do some fly fishing, even though you haven't practiced casting yet, remember that you can have fun and catch fish by trolling streamers or wet flies while you paddle. Canoes, kayaks, and jonboats will all work fine—without trolling motors and expensive gear. Let out your line and troll your flies slowly past good shoreline cover and drop-offs in small lakes and ponds, or in sheltered coves of larger waters.

22. Try Bank Fishing With Poles—Yes . . . *Poles*!

As the British have known for centuries, sitting on the bank with a long pole and fishing with hook, line, and bobber is as relaxing and productive a way of fishing as you can enjoy. You don't need a great deal of money, and you can do it on lakes, ponds, rivers, and streams. The popular image of this type of fishing is of the southerner fishing with a long canepole. The best way to go about it, however, is with today's long graphite rods and poles, available through tackle outfitters such Cabelas and Bass Pro Shops. These beautiful sticks come in lengths out to 16 feet, plenty long enough for you to hoist your bait out from the bank, even over

the tops of bushes. You can add a reel and have yourself a rig that can easily flip or toss your bait into productive water.

23. Bank Fishing: Working the *Real* Hotspots

Bank-fishing spots that offer open views of the water, and where the brush has been worn down by other anglers, are inviting and may, or may not, be good places to fish. The real hotspots, however, are the tough places to fish, the ones the crowds never touch. Watch for good holes and runs of water beyond the screens of bushes and tangled bank vegetation. Use crappie rods or long graphite poles that come in lengths to 16 feet. Wear knee-high rubber boots so you can maneuver freely. Reach out and drop your bait into water most people never fish.

24. The Fish-Catching Method Banned in Tournaments

Does trolling catch fish? It's a method banned in most tournaments. I guess it would create chaos among the boats, but it would also show the pros where the fish are. Enough said?

25. Plastic Tubs Can Hold Your Gear

Those plastic tubs commonly used for carrying laundry can be a great asset for your fishing. Use them in your boat and vehicle to hold your waders and other gear and tackle in organized, separate compartments. They're easy to put into your vehicle and to put away when your outing is over. Your truck and home don't get wet or muddy.

26. The Joys of Night Fishing

My brother is a private pilot who never flies at night. I asked him why? "It's because you can't see anything," he said, laughing. Well, that's not exactly true. You can see lots of things when your eyes become accustomed to the dark. And you can hear plenty, if you're listening: a fox barking, an owl hooting, ducks and geese

passing overhead, the splashes of marauding fish on the prowl. No, don't knock night fishing until you've tried it.

27. Great Maps Show the Way

As a confessed map junkie, I cannot resist poring over them every chance I get, dreaming of the trails to great fishing in the backcountry. Some of the best topo versions are the DeLorme's Topo USA. GPS users will find them a helpful way to download a track.

28. Taking a Kid Fishing—Tip One

My good friend Tom Hennessey, a writer and painter of great renown, as well as the outdoor editor of the *Bangor Daily News,* is a down-to-earth, no-nonsense man whose advice you can take to the bank. In his wonderful book, *Feathers 'n Fins,* The Amwell Press (1989), Tom wrote some tips on taking a kid fishing that are the best I've ever read, and Tom has graciously allowed us to reprint

them in full excerpts from his book. Four tips on taking a kid fishing may seem a bit much, but I don't think so. The tips are that good; the subject is that important. Although Tom used the word "boy" as a generic name, his tips apply to girls as well. If there is a kid out there whom you know and would like to take fishing, consider these words of wisdom, starting with Tip One:

"Keep in mind, kids are kids. Names of far-flung fishing grounds don't impress them. Neither do top-of-the-line rods and reels, or boats that cost as much as the first house you bought. What impresses them is being with you—and catching a fish or two . . . . In short forget about fishing and, for one day—his day—think about guiding . . . Accordingly, take your 'sport' fishing in a place where you know his rigging will tighten up frequently. That's the secret."

29. Taking a Kid Fishing—Tip Two

"It's not the end of the world if your boy tips the bait bucket over, or drops your tacklebox. Tell me you haven't. You know he'll step on your flyline, sit on the knapsack containing the sandwiches, lose his paddle in the swiftest part of the stream, and leave the insect repellent on a rock back where you put in. And you can bet your best reel that sometime during the day he'll go in over his boots—but won't dump them out until he's back in the canoe. Years later, you'll laugh at all that. Why not laugh at it then? It'll mean more."

—Tom Hennessey, *Feathers 'n Fins,*
The Amwell Press, 1989

30. Taking a Kid Fishing—Tip Three

"A boy's curiosity and competitive nature make him an eager student. You'll be surprised at how quickly he'll learn knots, the names of flies and lures, and how to rig tackle. If he were half as attentive in school, he'd be on the honor roll. The courses offered in the classroom of the great outdoors are, however, infinitely more interesting and challenging, and the teachers far less demanding."

—Tom Hennessey, *Feathers 'n Fins,*
The Amwell Press, 1989

31. The Deadly "Yo-Yo" Retrieve (Don't Miss This One!)

In a landmark article in the November-December 1996 issue of *Fly Rod & Reel* magazine, the late Gary LaFontaine described in detail one of the most important techniques discovered in his entire career. Due to a mix-up, he was sold a sinking fly line instead of a floating version when he was a young man going after smallmouth bass. Without noticing the kind of new fly line he was using, he tied his favorite floating Gerbubble deerhair bug to a long leader. After his initial amazement that his bug was sinking as the line pulled it toward the bottom, he started catching serious amounts of smallmouths. He let the line go to the bottom, and used a slow retrieve, with the floating fly riding just off the bottom. The technique is deadly, with a combination of sinking lines and floating bugs and long leaders. In trout fishing, particularly lakes, the results proved to be the same. LaFontaine later experimented with scuba divers watching the line, leader, and floating fly do their thing underwater. He discovered that the line, scraping across the bottom, was churning up all kinds of trout "goodies." In other words, the line was creating a chum line for the trout.

32. Don't Miss Prime Time

As the sun is setting and the shadows deepening, the idea of heading home or to camp before darkness descends is perfectly natural. By doing so, however, you might miss out on the day's best fishing time—those precious minutes between sunset and darkness. That's when fish will be on the move, more likely to strike than at any time since dawn. If your gear includes a small flashlight or headlamp, you'll have no reason to dread the dark. Keep on fishing! It may pay off between sunset and darkness.

33. Houseboat Fishing: What a Great Idea

Imagine being with your family or a bunch of friends on a comfortable, easy-to-steer-and-run boat that chugs along anywhere you want to go on big waters like the TWA lakes, the

Boundary Waters area of Minnesota and Ontario, or the high desert lakes of the West. You're not just out for a swim or a boat ride here: You're going fishing. Big time! Along with the houseboat that you'll live on, you'll also have a good fishing boat in tow. Consider the houseboat as your movable base camp. You can stop and fish anywhere you please, and in the evenings pull into quiet coves for a relaxing dinner and night anchored in a safe spot. The Internet, of course, is one place to make this kind of fishing vacation start to happen. Check out www.houseboating.org.

34. Got Any Clouser Minnows?

"In fact, the Clouser minnow has probably been the most popular fly designed in the last fifteen years. It's still useful in both fresh  and salt water and appropriate for any type of fish. It offers size flexibility; that is, it can be effective at 10 inches long or 1 inch long. By adjusting the weight of the eyes you can customize the swimming depth of the fly. I have to date caught eighty-six species of fish on versions of that lure, about a third of which were caught using a combination of either chartreuse and yellow or chartreuse and white on the wing."

—Lefty Kreh, with Chris Millard,
My Life Was THIS BIG and Other True Fishing Tales, Skyhorse Publishing, 2008

35. Casting: The Real Art of Fishing

No matter what kind of fishing you're doing, making a good cast has a huge bearing on the results. Other than dropping your bait straight over the side, putting your lure, fly, or even live-bait rig into a precise spot is critical. Almost always, the best casters are the best fishermen. Spend as much time practicing your casting on your lawn or a nearby lake as you possibly can, and you'll catch more fish and enjoy your fishing a lot more.

36. Understanding the Thermocline

"A 'thermocline' is a layer of water that usually develops in reservoirs during the summer where the temperature rapidly falls with an increase in depth. Water temperatures above and below the thermocline change more gradually. Because there is often little oxygen below the thermocline, it is generally accepted that fishing is frequently poor below this layer."

—Oklahoma Department of Wildlife Conservation,
"Reservoir Fishing Tips,"
www.wildlifedepartment.com/fishing.htm

37. The Backlash Retrieve: Deadliest in All Fishing

If you had $1 for every fish that has been hooked—quite unexpectedly—while an angler was trying to untangle the line on his reel after a backlash, you'd be very wealthy. Backlashes with baitcasting tackle and tangled line with spinning divert the angler's attention long enough for the lure being used to sink all the way to the bottom. Then, when the retrieve finally begins, bottom-hugging fish zero in for a strike. There's a lesson here, but most anglers never heed it. Simply allow your jig or bait to sink all the way to the bottom, however agonizingly long it takes, then slowly ease it up while twitching it a little. You'll catch lots of fish.

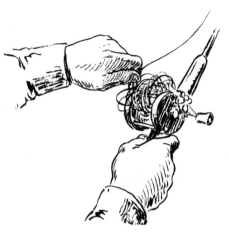

38. The Dock That Produces More Fish

If you can find a dock that sits alone, providing the only shade and cover in the area, you might be onto something special. Look for bass, panfish, and pickerel to be waiting in the dark waters.

39. Betting on the Outside Bend

In most river situations, at any significant curve in the river's flow, it's the outside bend you should give special time and attention. The push of all the water against the turn can dig out undercut banks and holes where fish will be waiting in ambush for prey.

40. The Windy Side Is Where You Want to Be

Although it seems perfectly natural to seek the calm and quiet water of the lee side of the lake when the wind is blowing, you ought to be doing just the opposite. Fish the windy side, hard. Bait will be blown against the windy shore and pinned there, and the fish will be feeding in those waters.

41. It's Not Just the Lure

No matter how effective the lure or bait you're using is supposed to be, there's a lot more to fishing it well than merely casting it out and reeling it back. Use your imagination, think about what you can be doing to the lure to make it look alive. Fast, slow, wiggling, shaking, stopping, dipping, sinking: Put your mind out there in the water where the bait is and put it to work for you.

42. Use the Deadly Slingshot Cast in Tight Places

One of the best casts when using fly tackle doesn't look like a cast at all, but can catch fish for you when no one else is catching a thing. In places on streams or lakes where brush makes it impossible to get a cast into one of those shady, dark holes where you just know a fish is waiting, try the Slingshot Cast. Ease into and lean over

the brush as carefully as you can. Slowly get your rod pointed out over or through the brush toward your target. With the fly or bug in your hand and your line the same length as the rod, pull back smartly, get a nice bow in the rod tip, and let it fly. You can hook a lot of fish with this sneaky tactic. Your problem will be playing them, once they're on. You may end up getting wet, but that's fishing.

—James A. Henshall, MD, *Book of the Black Bass*, 1881

43. Why Suspended Fish Are Tough

When walleyes, bass, and panfish are suspended, holding at a certain depth where oxygen levels and water temperature suit them just right, working your lure at exactly the right depth becomes critical—and difficult to do. Lures that yo-yo up and down through the critical zone won't be as effective as those that swim and fish at one level. That's a reason trolling is so effective for suspended fish.

44. When Snagged Lures Snap Loose

When your lure is snagged on a tree trunk or stump above the water, pulling it as hard as you can in a direct line with your position on the bank, or your boat, is asking for big trouble. If the lure pops loose, it and all those treble hooks will be flying your way as if shot from a gun. Somebody is going to get hurt. To free a lure when you think such a dangerous moment is possible, take the time to get over to the lure and pry it loose.

45. Riding High, Down Deep

At the Cabelas site, www.cabelas.com, the Todd's Wiggle Minnow is listed under the Warm Water section of Fly Fishing. This
is a foam-bodied floater for bass and pike on the surface. What
I like about it, however, is that it's a perfect fly for the bottoms-
up fly-fishing trick we've covered earlier. Use a sinking fly line,
or heavy fly such as a Czech nymph, with 7 feet or so of leader
attached to your Wiggle Minnow. It will ride behind and above
your line or weight pulled over the bottom. You'll catch fish.

46. The Fly-Rod Grip That Sets More Hooks

When your fly or bug is on the water, grip your fly rod by sliding your thumb down the side and allowing all your knuckles to show on top—as opposed to a grip more like a handshake. When you get a strike, simply roll you knuckles back to the right and you lift the rod tip as you pull on the line. You'll set more hooks this way.

47. Baitcasting: Hand Position for Better Casting

It may look funny from the side, but the proper position for the reel when making a cast with a baitcasting rod and reel is to have your hand turned to the left and the handles of the reel on top of the spool in a perpendicular position. The reel will turn with less friction, and your wrist will be looser, delivering easier power.

48. Casting Sink-Tip and Full-Sinking Lines

You can't pull sink-tip and full-sinking lines out of the water and get a decent backcast. They must be retrieved and be almost completely out of the water before you begin your cast and shoot them out again.

49. Fish Jigs for Spring Panfish

For crappies, bluegills, and perch, fish tiny jigs with soft-plastic grubs deep and slow. Let them sink until you find the bottom, then adjust the sink-depth to avoid the weeds and/or lighten up your jig size and weight. Remember that these baits, with their fluttering action, are fishing for you on the way down as well as when being retrieved. Cabelas and Bass Pro Shops have zillions of them. I like yellow and white best.

50. Where to Fish Early, Pre-Spawn Bass

Expect largemouth bass to be moving onto flats and lake edges that catch the sun early and often. (They're as tired of Old

Man Winter as you are.) Fish the headwaters where rivers and creeks flow into impoundments. These tributaries will warm up before the main, colder lake waters. Bass move into the areas fed by the warming flow of waters. Be there to meet them with swim baits, such as Berkley's soft-plastic Gulp Minnows and Mann's Hard-Nosed Jerkbaits. There are many other swimbait choices to check out at Cabelas or Bass Pro Shops. Many experienced and well-known anglers prefer crankbaits for this type fishing. I do not. I've found they're tough to fish with the slow action I want at this time of the year. Fish swimbaits very, very slowly.

51. Don't Waste Time on Early-Season Top Water

Despite some exceptions, it's a mistake to spend your fishing hours searching for top-water action in early season. Sure, we all want top-water action when we can get it, but on these first cold spring outings, I'll go down (even deep!) for action and fish.

52. Watch Those Weather Fronts

When you're having one of those springtime "teaser" spells of warming weather for two or three days, and a new cold front is predicted to be moving in, try to fish just before the front arrives. In a posting on Cabelas Web site, "Contending with Spring Weather Fronts," pro bass expert Denny Brauer says several days of consistent, warming weather should give you the best springtime fishing.

After the next cold front passes, fishing will be tougher, with the fish holding tighter to cover or in deep water. Fish your crankbaits, jigs, or worms much slower now, in the cover, or outside on channels, drop-offs, creek beds, and points. "The jig is probably the best for this situation because the lure's at its best in the springtime after the passage of a cold front."

53. Use Gulp Baits for Spring Action

Berkley's Gulp soft-plastic baits come in a variety of forms, sizes, and colors. Two are on the top of my go-to tactics for spring. For mixed-bag action on everything from crappies to bass, use the 2-inch Gulp Minnow Grub on 1/16- or 1/8-ounce jigs. I prefer the yellow or the white. Let 'em sink, swim, or jerk them very slowly.

For more action when bass are the targets, fish the Gulp 3-inch Minnow in yellow/green or white.

54. Fine-Tuning Your Jigging Techniques

If you aren't getting any strikes jigging spring waters for panfish or bass using some of the techniques outlined above, try jigging slower and deeper until you find the fish. If you've had trouble getting your bait into the strike zones on a consistent basis, consider buying a reel with a line-counter system that lets you know how deep your jig is fishing every time.

55. It's Woolly Buggers for Spring Trout

When there's no hatch to match, and the water is running high, cold, and off-color—and you're on fly-fishing-only water—you can bet your day's fishing on an olive Woolly Bugger fished slow and deep. Choose a bead-head model large enough to get down to the fish. You may prefer the jazzed-up crystal Bugger, but make no mistake: Nothing catches spring trout like a well-fished Woolly Bugger.

56. Nervous Water Means Action

When a patch of water seems to be shimmering or jiggling, while all the water around it is calm, it may not be a gust of wind hitting it. You might have a nervous water situation, with tiny baitfish struggling on the surface to escape the predators zeroing in for the kill. Get your bait into the water now!

57. Live Bait in Current: Let It Ride

When bobber fishing with live bait in a stream, if your bobber goes under, but there's no hook-up when you react, don't pull in your line and bait. Instead, let out more line and let the bobber float on downstream a bit. Chances are the interested fish will hit your bait again, before it escapes.

58. When the Wind's in Your Favor

When your boat is positioned on the side of a lake, or when you're fishing from shore, and you've got a strong wind in your face, consider yourself lucky. Microorganisms are carried downwind by the push of the water, tiny baitfish follow, and the larger fish are right behind them. Look for fishing to be best on the *downwind* reaches of the lake.

59. Ready for Action? Go to Drop-Shot Fishing

The Drop-Shot methods that have been the rage in bass fishing for some time now can not only help you catch more bass, but panfish, walleyes, and other species as well. They work because they get your lure or bait down to where the fish are. The rig and techniques are many and varied, but at its simplest form, you tie on a swivel clip weight between $^1/_{16}$- to ¼-ounce, the clip giving you the ability to change the weight as you wish to experiment in getting down. Tie a Palomer Knot about 12 to 14 inches above the weight, leaving the tag (loop) end rather open. Pull the tag end around and through the hook eye to keep the bait or lure straight. The hook should be pointed up and on the rod tip side of the line. Most anglers fish the rig in a vertical jigging fashion, but you can also cast it out, let it sink, and fish it back along the bottom. Many anglers prefer to make the business end of the rig a leader, say 6- to 8-pound test, when their line seems too big for finesse fishing.

60. Self-Propelled, Go-Anywhere Fishing Crafts

Somewhere between sitting on a stool on the bank, floating comfortably with a professional-type float boat, and racing about the lakes in a $30,000 bass boat, a form of fishing has evolved and is spreading like wildfire. Fishing from kayaks, float tubes, and kick-boats has turned angling for everything from bluegills to blue-finned tuna into fishing adventure and freedom. These crafts are affordable, can be stowed with ease, and are immensely portable. Once launched on the water of your choice, they allow you to fish with stealth and precision, working the holes, depths, and structure that bank anglers can't reach, and the big boats barely explore, before they race away. Fishing methods that may once have been considered offbeat and extreme are now the subjects of Web sites, books, DVDs, and clubs.

61. Float Tubes Become U-Boats

Float tubes—often called belly boats—for fishing have been around so long that they have evolved into veritable fishing machines far advanced from the original doughnuts that were used in the pioneering days of float-tube angling. Today's tubes have strong, puncture-free covers shaped in the form of a U for better entry and exiting—and also for faster movement. The tubes are loaded with storage pockets for tackle and refreshments, and even back rests and rod holders. The kick-fins have been modernized to be stronger, and are either floatable or come with safety straps to prevent loss. Stow your gear, pull on your waders (preferably neoprene if it's going to be chilly or cold), and away you go for fishing adventure in hard-to-reach spots the crowds never touch. Sites like www.basspro.com and www.cabelas.com are loaded with products and accessories you need to get into this exciting fishing.

62. The Knot Book That Has Them All

Every knot you can imagine for fishing—both fresh and salt water—is shown in graphic, easy-to-follow steps in Lindsey Philpott's *The Complete Book of Fishing Knots, Leaders, and Lines*, Skyhorse (2009).

Of all the knot instruction books I've ever seen—and I think I've seen them all—Philpott's is the most useful. Buy it at Amazon and other sites and practice the knots you need until you master them. If you're serious about your fishing, this is one book you want in your bookcase.

63. Knots for the Braided Superlines

The correct knots for using with the braided superlines—such as FireLine, SpiderWire, Tuf-Line, and others—have sometimes provided fuel for Internet discussions. In particular, there have been recommendations to use the Palomar knot for tying on your hook or lure, and to avoid the usually popular and widely used Improved Cinch Knot.

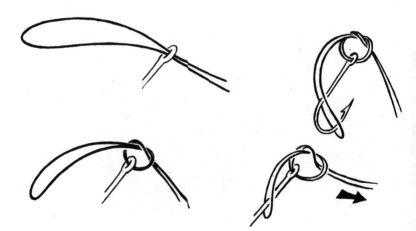

64. Tighten Down Those Fluorocarbon Leader Knots

Fluorocarbon lines and leaders are stronger and less visible (and cost more) than anything in traditional nylon. Fluorocarbon knots are stronger, but they do not absorb water as nylon does, tightening the knot by swelling. You, the angler, must pull the fluorocarbon knots as tight as possible.

65. Tying on a Hook—the Improved Clinch Knot

Whether it's the best or not is arguable among experts and guides, but the Improved Clinch Knot is the most popular way of tying on a hook. Wet the knot before pulling it tight.

66. The Loop That Gives Your Lure Action

The Duncan Loop is a more advanced way of tying on a hook or lure than the Improved Clinch Knot. The Loop allows your lure to swing and dance, giving it enticing action.

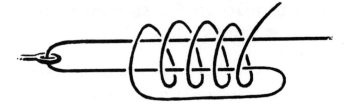

67. Looping a Fly Line to a Leader Loop

When both your leader and fly lines have loops, they should join together without tying problems. Some anglers still don't get it right, however. Here's how to join the two loops for better fishing.

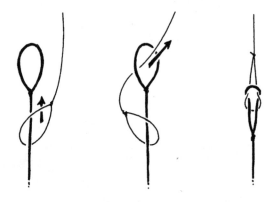

68. How to Join Leader Sections, Part One: The Blood Knot

Okay, your leader has been cut or broken so many times that it's too short for the kind of fishing you're doing. Now you need to add tippet material. The Blood Knot is the way to go for a smooth, powerful connection. Some anglers—like those with frozen fingers or arthritis in their fingers—find this one difficult to tie. In fact, there are gizmos you can buy to make the job easier.

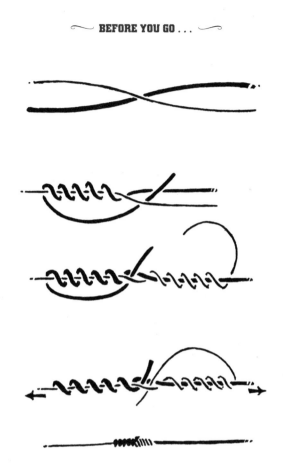

Here's how it's done. By the way, if you're trying to join line sections of mismatched sizes, you're in for a tough time unless you're very, very good at this.

69. How to Join Leader Sections, Part Two: The Surgeon's Knot

If you're not up to the Blood Knot for joining leader or line sections, the Surgeon's Knot will probably get the job done for you. Surgeon's Knot is a polite term for a good old Granny Knot.

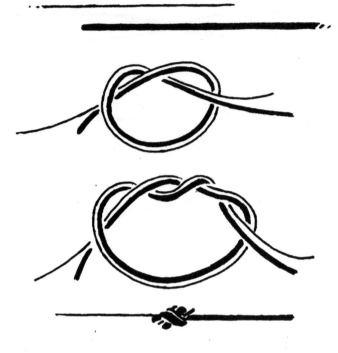

70. The Loop You Need for Drop Shot Fishing

The Perfection Loop has been around a long time, but today it's coming more into play, particularly in bass and walleye fishing, because you need this loop to attach a lure to your line above your sinker. The bottom of your line doesn't have to be attached to a sinker; it could be tied to a second jig. [Editor's Note: An alternate way of tying a lure or fly to the line was developed by the great angler and filmmaker Glenn Lau. See Homer Circle's article in the Panfish Section.]

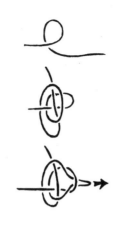

71. The Knot Atlantic Salmon Fishers Swear By

Veteran Atlantic salmon anglers like my friend Tom Hennessey, author, painter, and columnist for the *Bangor Daily News*, and

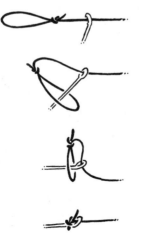

Stanley Bogdan, the famous reel maker, do not like conventional knots for their Atlantic salmon flies. They insist that the fly not wobble or twist, but remain in a dead-straight pull with the leader. They get it with the Improved Turle Knot.

72. Add a Loop to Your Leader or Line

Your leader or line didn't come with a loop, but you want one. You can get it by tying the Surgeon's Loop.

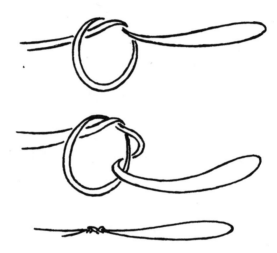

73. Connecting Fly Line to Leader Without Loops: Tube Nail Knot

If you're not connecting your fly line and leader by the loop-to-loop method, you're going to need the Nail Knot. It's not that hard to master if you take your time and practice.

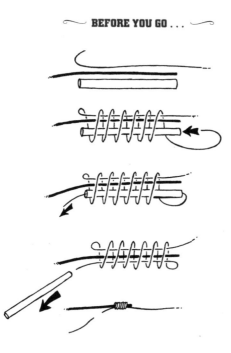

74. The No Tube Fly Line Connection: The Needle Nail Knot

"No tube," you say. Well, can you find a needle? This will work just fine and give you a strong, smooth, snag-proof connection.

CHAPTER 2

Largemouth & Smallmouth Bass

75. My Most Important Bass Fishing Lesson

It took a lot of casts, and a lot of years, and a lot of wasted time before I finally grasped the most important lesson in largemouth bass fishing: You *must* fish weedless lures and baits. You will occasionally catch bass alongside cover with lures using exposed hooks, but the majority of your strikes will come when you fish your lure right among the stumps, limbs, lily pads, and weedy holes. Sure, open-water fishing is more visual and less work, but do you want to catch bass or do you just want to mess around?

76. Top-Water Patience Can Pay

You're probably familiar with the surface lure tactic of letting your lure lie motionless on the water after it splashes down—at least until the ripples spread out and die away. There's another method—requiring infinitely more patience—that sometimes pays big dividends: Let your lure lie still for about three minutes, then jiggle it every so slightly. Then jiggle it some more, and eventually start it moving very, very slowly. You might be surprised by what happens.

77. They're *Not Hitting* Because They're *Not There!*

As pointed out elsewhere in this book, when a stretch of shoreline that has been producing good fishing suddenly goes cold, the usual angling lament is, "They've stopped biting." Other stretches of shoreline are deemed to be poor because they seldom or never produce fish. The key thing to remember about the "good" stretches of shoreline is that when the fish "aren't biting," they probably have moved out along their migration routes to deeper water. Turning your back on the shoreline and exploring outside water, using charts, electronics, and local knowledge (if it is available), should lead to better catches when they're "not biting" along your favorite, dependable shorelines.

78. Finding Those Disappearing Bass

Fish finders, GPS units, and other devices, coupled with sophisticated boats and motors and a new knowledge of fishing honey holes in the vast waters of lakes and reservoirs, has lead not only

to tournaments and halcyon days for cashing in on exploding tackle demands, but to the notion that would have made our grandfathers faint: "Turn you back on the shore . . . get out in the lake . . . that's where the fish are."

79. A Creature of Habits

A bass caught in Texas or Georgia has virtually the same habits as one caught in Ohio or Pennsylvania. Their individual traits and preferences don't make a dime's bit of difference in terms of their needs in differing parts of the country. They all need food, cover, oxygen, and bottom cover they can relate to while feeding, moving, or hiding. The timing of their various activities may differ from place to place, but the way they go about their lives is virtually the same.

80. She—Not He—Is the Big One That Got Away

Anglers invariably call fish "He," but in the world of bass, the females are the biggest fish. When an angler says, "He got away!" he probably should have said, "*She* got away!"

81. Suspended Bass—They're Tough to Catch

When bass are holding, suspended at mid-water levels, with no baitfish near them, they sometimes can seem to be locked in those positions all day. You see them on your depth finder, but they seem to have little interest in your deep-running lures. As a last-ditch effort, try jigging for them, straight down.

82. Summer's Smallmouth Dividends

Tired of getting skunked on your favorite trout waters during high summer? Then turn your fly and light spinning rods toward the smallmouth rivers. You'll find plenty of action from battling fish that are as strong and jump as much as any trout you ever saw.

83. Fishing Flooded Timber: Rule One

All flooded timber looks inviting to the bass angler. All that cover, all those shadows for bass to hide in and wait for prey. But when you're looking at hundreds—or thousands—of acres of flooded timber, you soon realize the fish aren't scattered throughout. They are not lying in wait behind every tree. Instead, as in other lakes, they relate to bottom contours. The timber near the right bottom contours and channels will be the timber that holds the fish. Think *bottom contours and conditions* first. *Timber*, second.

84. Targeting Docks and Bridge Pilings

Those shadowy docks and bridge pilings always look like great cover for fish. And they are! Bass, all kinds of panfish, pickerel,

pike, even walleyes are probably lurking there. You'll catch more fish at docks or pilings by getting your boat into position and making your first casts parallel to the target. Cast in toward the bank and run your lure alongside the dock—as close to the boards as you can get it—back to the boat. Next, if there's room under the dock, try skipping side-arm casts to get your lure under the boards into the shadows.

85. Fish Rip-Raps for Early Spring Bass

Cold-water early spring bass can be tough to catch, but one way to cut the odds, says pro Timmy Horton, is to fish rip-raps—those rocky barriers supporting roads across lakes and reservoirs and dams along ponds. The rocks heat up with the warming spring sun, and the fish move into the adjacent waters. They can be on the rocks or as far as 30 feet outside. Especially good are the breaks in the rip-rap where boats can slide through. Horton likes jerkbaits for this fishing, and goes deep with the longer-bill models. Vary your retrieve from sudden jerks, to smooth pulls, to slow twitches. You'll catch bass, Horton says, on his "The Bass Pro" feature on the Versus Country Internet site.

86. Bass Fishing's Super-Rig: It's Famous Because It Works

If you seriously want to catch bass—and not simply enjoy a nice day on the water—then sooner or later you're going to have to fish plastic worms or other soft-plastic baits. Yes, worm fishing makes some anglers yawn. Yes, it's tough to get the hang of, requiring

patience and the development of all-important feel and touch. But the tactic catches bass, lots of them, big ones and little ones. Sometimes it catches them on days when nothing else works.

87. How to Set Up the Texas Rig

The rig starts with your favorite worm or soft-plastic bait, a worm hook, and a bullet-type sinker in a size to take you deep or shallow as you prefer for the location and conditions. First, pass the line through the slip sinker and tie on the hook. Second, push the point of the hook into the center of the end of the worm head and thread it about ½ inch into the center of the worm body. Next, bring the point of the hook out of the body. It should be about

½ inch back from the head. Now pull the eye and shank of the hook back through the worm body until the eye end of the hook disappears into the worm about ¼ inch. Lastly, push the point of the hook into the worm just past the barb. Now you have a straight worm that's virtually weedless.

88. The Deadly Carolina Rig

The ubiquitous Texas Rig is rivaled by the Carolina Rig for bass-catching effectiveness. Basically, the Carolina Rig differs by having the bullet sinker positioned up the line, instead of on the nose of the soft bait as in the Texas. This makes the soft-plastic lure or worm sink slower and float behind and above the bullet sinker. The lure or worm moves freely with an enticing action. The Carolina Rig is so effective that many top anglers never bother to use the Texas Rig at all. Many tournament anglers keep one rod loaded for action with a Carolina Rig all set up.

89. A Really Good Bass Bait

The YUM Money Minnows, from www.lurenet.com and tackle dealers, have been attracting a lot of attention from pro bassers. I now have them in my own tackle box and can report great success in using them, especially in the "Sight-Fishing" episodes covered elsewhere in the bass section of this book. I've been using the 3 ½-inch version in bluegill colors, but there are plenty of others to choose from. Rig it Texas style with an extra-wide-gap, offset worm hook or a shank-weighted swimbait hook—and make it weedless. The lure has a belly slot. I turn the hook up through it and out the top of the bait, then set the hook lightly into the back to make it weedless. Good instructions for using the weighted hook and getting the lure deeper are on the www. lurenet.com site. My personal use with this lure has me convinced that you'll catch more bass by using it.

90. The Floating Worm: Fun and Good

Floating plastic worms, made to stay on top or sink far slower than normal plastic worms, have arrived in bass fishing with a big-bucks bang, winning tournaments here and there and catching bass for anglers who like topwater fishing. Bass Pro Shops, www.basspro.com, carries them in their own brand, the Gambler brand, and two types of floating worms by Berkley Gulp. You should check other sites as well, remembering that not all plastic worms are true floaters. Rig them Texas-style, with a 3/0 light wire hook, a small swivel, and 12 to 15 inches of leader.

91. Skipping Floating Worms

Do you know how to skip a floating worm? You should, it's fun— just like skipping rocks on the water when you were a kid—and you catch lots of bass to boot. Picture a deep, dark lair back under some overhanging trees, or under a dock. The only way you can get a worm in there is to skip it over the water like a flat rock. It's not hard to do with a floating worm. Practice it on open water until you get the touch. Then start skipping your floating worm back in there where the bass are waiting.

92. Working Early-Spring's Deadliest Lure

When bass are staging for the spawn on breaklines from 4 to 8 feet deep, close to deeper water, pro guide Troy Jens of Lake Guntersville, Alabama, likes to go after them with the Cotton Cordell Super Spot. He uses the ½-ounce Super Spot and works it just fast enough to stay above the bottom. One reason he likes the bait is because it can be fished from very slow to super fast. Writing for the Web site www.lurenet.com, Jens says he uses the Super Spot from ice-out through water temperatures in the 40s. "As the water warms into the 50s, I begin fishing the tops of the humps and ledges and I begin moving further back into the creeks."

93. Floating Worms: Make Sure They Can

Not all plastic worms are real floaters. The genuine floaters are chemically designed and made to resist sinking. They do sink, but very, very slowly, and they ride above the sinker when pulled along the bottom—even when attached to a hook. Make sure you're getting the real deal, real floating worms.

94. Hooking Up Your Floating Worms

If the hook you use on a floating worm is too heavy, you'll be defeating the reason you are using a floater. A 3/0 or 2/0 that's thin and wire-like should be just right. Drive the hook through the worm, then back it up to make it weedless.

95. Smallmouths on the Rocks

In his wonderful autobiography, *My Life Was THIS BIG and Other True Fishing Tales*, Skyhorse Publishing (2008), by Lefty Kreh with Chris Millard, Lefty not only points out the importance of fishing the rocks to catch river smallmouths, he puts a great deal of emphasis on the angle of the cast. Presenting the fly from the wrong side of the rock will not result in strikes because of the unnatural drift of the fly (much the same as in "drag" in presenting trout flies). For instance, a rock with current on both sides will fish better when the cast and the drifting fly are on the same side as the current. A fly cast across the rock to reach the current on the other side usually will not work.

96. Reaction Strikes: Take 'Em When You Can

When bass are on the feed, searching for food like predators on the prowl, they are, of course, striking out of hunger. But many strikes occur when the bass is just sitting there, finning easily, not feeding at all. A case in point might be a bass lying under a log, or in a stretch of lily pads. A crankbait or other lure that suddenly flashes past sometimes elicits a savage strike that comes out of pure instinct to attack available prey. It's as if your lure woke up a sleeping bass. It doesn't happen all the time, but when it does, count yourself as fortunate.

97. Sight Fishing for Largemouths—Step One

As the great Yogi Berra once proclaimed, "You can observe a lot just by watching." Truer words were never spoken when it comes to largemouth bass fishing. When the water is still and quiet—usually early in the morning or at dusk, especially in late spring or early fall—the sight and sound of minnows on the move mean bass are in attack mode. Those minnows aren't just playing around. They're about to be gulped into a bigmouth's gullet, and they're trying to leave Dodge. Sometimes you'll even hear or see the bass slash into the school, or see big swirls. Your tackle should be ready for the next step.

98. Sight Fishing for Largemouths—Step Two

Your electric motor has just ceased humming, or you've carefully laid down your canoe paddle. You're drifting into the area where you saw or heard minnows on the run, or a bass swirl or strike. Your chosen lure (which we'll cover in Step Three) is ready. Ahead of you are lily pads, half-sunken logs, or a brush-choked shoreline. Here, in this moment and position, is where most anglers fail. Either they move too aggressively and spook the fish, or they make casts that are too far out in the open water. They're thinking the bass will come roaring out of the cover and strike. While it's true that sometimes happens, don't count on it. The cast must go as close to the cover, or even into it with a weedless bait, as possible. Right here is where casting ability shines. Putting that bait right into every nook and cranny is the key to getting a strike.

99. Sight Fishing for Largemouths—Step Three

There are about a zillion lures that will catch fish in this situation, but I have a couple of favorites, and it's my book, so here we go: I'm positively in love with two soft-plastic baits in the swimbait or jerk bait category. (No, I do not get them for free. I buy them, like you.) The Mann Hardnose and the Strike King Zulu have been absolute killers for me and my buddies in sight-fishing situations. Actually, they're good baits all the time. You can swim them and jerk them and expect savage strikes. We fish them with the Texas Rig, minus the sinker for the sight-fishing situations. With the hook embedded properly, they're virtually weedless. As with other recommendations, check Bass Pro Shops and Cabela's.

100. Time to Walk the Dog

Everybody wants to catch bass with topwater lures—and why not? When conditions are right, and bass are feeding on or near the surface, there's nothing like the explosive strike of an aggressive bass. You can fish topwater lures many ways, including the famous "Walk the Dog" technique of slowly working it over the surface. You can pause it, twitch it, or just let it lie there, waiting. Then slowly move it a foot or so, then pause, wait, and twitch once again. When the strike comes, you will know it!

101. Proven Topwater Lures

When the time and conditions are right for topwater fishing, the seven lures featured here are the ones you can absolutely count on to get strikes. Yes, there are others, endless numbers of them, and if you're willing to experiment, you'll probably find a new favorite or two among them. But these are my topwater best bets. I have seen them in action and witnessed them being used by many expert anglers. There are many topwater lures out there that are far less expensive than these. Quite frankly, in my opinion, they are not as good. These are the best. Fish them and have fun!

1. Rapala Skitter Pop

An absolute killer bait from the famous maker of wooden lures. This was Rapala's first-ever topwater lure, and it's a great one. The plastic cupped lip produces a "spitting" action. An assortment of color finishes, 2 to 2 ¾ inches, at $7.99 from Cabela's as this is written. The Skitter Pop will catch both largemouth and smallmouth bass wherever they swim. Available at www.cabelas.com.

2. Rebel Zell Rowland Pop-R

Moving down in price to $4.99 from Bass Pro Shops is this popular plastic bait, aka "The Pop-R King." Many good anglers who don't want to fork over the extra buck for the wooden Rapala fish the Rebel Pop-R. In four color finishes, at 2 ½ inches, the Pop-R is a lure you can count on. Available at www.basspro.com.

3. Arbogast Hula Popper

A favorite for decades—because it works. When the Hula Popper doesn't get strikes from surface feeders, you're probably in for a very slow day of surface action. You can pop it, walk it, let it rest, and tremble it. It comes in a variety of finishes. Costs $4.99 at Cabela's.

4. Heddon Lucky 13 and Baby Lucky 13

Created in 1920, the Lucky 13 has been catching bass ever since. Today's versions, the Lucky 13 (3 ¾ inches) and Baby Lucky 13 (2 5/8inches), produce resonating sound and a weaving body action for a variety of gamefish, especially bass. Cabela's lists both at $4.99. Fish the Baby version for smallmouths.

5. Arbogast Jitterbug

This lure has been a mainstay in the tackleboxes of bass addicts for decades. The back-and-forth, plodding, popping action represents live prey struggling, and bass on the feed gobble it with fury. It costs $4.69 to $4.99, and comes in 2- and 3-inch sizes, in a variety of colors. As with several other topwater baits, failure to get strikes with a Jitterbug does not bode well for your surface fishing that day.

6. Heddon Zara Spook, Super Spook, and Super Spook Jr.

Heddon's Zara Spook was one of the first—if not *the* first—topwater, Walk the Dog lures. It's still catching fish today, and costs $4.99 at Cabelas. The Super Spook is an upgraded version of the Zara, and at $4.99 is a solid choice for a variety of fish. The Spook Jr. is also $4.99 and is the choice for smallmouths and picky largemouths.

7. Lucky Craft Sammy

Ready to spend $10 for a single lure? If you're really hungry for topwater action, and nothing else seems to work, the Lucky Craft Sammy might save your day. At $9.99 (on sale) and $13.99 to $15.99 regularly priced (Cabela's), the Lucky Craft Sammy has a lot of new technology going for it and consistently gets strikes. If you can afford it, and are not afraid of losing it to a big fish or submerged log, give it a try. Comes in a variety of colors, 2 ½ to 4 inches.

102. Casting to Bass Cover

A cast that lands more than a foot away from bass cover is a wasted cast.

103. When the Water's Falling Too Fast

When fishing rivers for bass, especially big rivers, the periods after heavy rains when the water is falling ultrafast will often cause the bass to move out into the depths and suspend. They'll stay there until the flow stabilizes.

104. Double Your Fun With Two Jigs

Deep-jigging for smallmouths is always a reliable tactic, but don't forget to take the trouble to add a second jig to your line. Fish a heavier jig on the end of your line, with a lighter jig of another color attached to a dropper about 18 inches up the line. A Perfection Loop Knot will work nicely for the dropper, or some other type if you have a favorite. Don't be surprised to find yourself battling a pair of smallmouths at times. Sometimes a hooked bass creates a frenzy among its mates in a school.

105. Quick Pull, Then No Fish

What's going on when you feel a bass has picked up your worm, yet you set the hook on nothing but water? Chances are the bass simply grabbed the tail end of the worm to keep it from moving away, then dropped it as you tightened the line. The fish never sucked the worm into its mouth, because the angler kept it moving away too quickly.

106. Pre-Spawn Bass: More Strikes in the Afternoon

In the spring, as the water temps rise into the 50s at midday and during the afternoon, you should get more strikes from fish moving into warmer waters. On a cold morning when fishing is slow, if the water temps are slowly climbing, you can reasonably look forward to afternoon action. Don't go home at lunch.

107. Why Live Bait Catches Giant Bass

Live bait—such as shiners, minnows, and even sunfish—are such a deadly attractor to bass for two important reasons. First, and obvious, is the fact that they are the real prey bass are accustomed to feeding on. But equally important, and often overlooked by anglers who use them in open water, these live baits swim into and underneath thick pads and cover where big bass lurk and lures never go.

108. Your Best Chance for a Monster Bass

If you are fortunate enough to locate a hole where a big bass resides, your surest way to get the lunker will be using a live sunfish. Not too big, not too small, a 4-incher is about right. Hook it up top, at the dorsal fin, with a Number 6. Feed out line to let the bait swim into the hole . . . then wait.

109. Picking the Right Hook for Plastic Worms

Picking the right hook size for the plastic worm you're using is simple. Basically, it's big worm, big hook; small worm, small hook. For a 7- to 8-inch worm, a 3/0 or 4/0 hook will be just right, while a 1/0 will be too small and a 6/0 too big. For a 5- to 6-inch worm, use a 2/0 hook. For finesse worms under 5 inches, use 1 and 1/0. Now all you have to do is to make sure they're sharp.

110. The Single-Worm Trick for Bass

Bluegill and crappie anglers are sometimes surprised when the tug on their line turns out to be a hard-pulling, fighting largemouth bass in the 1- to 2-pound class. When bluegill fishing, you can make this unexpected treat happen more often by using a single earthworm hooked right through the middle. Set your float to let your worm dangle at various depths, and you'll catch a bass. I don't know why this single-worm trick works, but it does.

111. Coping With Surface Lure Splash-Down

While bass will sometimes strike lures the instant they hit the surface—and even grab them right out of the air—most bass-fishing experts put their faith in letting their surface plug or bug rest on the water a few moments before starting the retrieve. The theory is that the bait splashing down will frighten fish in the immediate vicinity, even make them swim off some distance. Let the bait sit until well after the ripples spread away and die out completely, then give the bait a twitch. Then do some more twitching. Then, as you retrieve, try slow crawls with wiggles, violent jerks and pops, or whatever seems to be working.

112. Good Bass Fishing Close to Home

Sometimes it's possible to ignore a lake that's close to your home, simply because it looks as if it's harboring too much activity. But when you really consider the people using the lake, and come to realize that they're mostly swimmers, kayakers, sailboaters, and float tubers—not fishermen—you may find you've got a good fishing spot all to yourself. Not on weekends, but during the week, especially at dawn.

113. If You're Not Drop-Shot Fishing . . .

If you haven't given drop-shot fishing a try yet, you're missing out on a great fishing technique. The variations on the technique are many, and you can have a lot of fun experimenting with them. Right here, however, I will keep it simple and explain a basic rig that will catch bass—not to mention walleyes and panfish—wherever you fish. Basically the rig is another wrinkle in the "Bottoms-Up" fishing trend. At the end of your line is a tungsten weight, say ¼ or ³/₈ ounce, hooked to the line with a snap swivel so you can change the weight as the depth demands. Tied with a palamar knot 12 inches or so up the line is a No. 2 Wide Gap hook. Put your worm or jig on that hook, and you're in business. You can add a swivel above the hook if you wish. Hook your worm through the nose or through the body wacky-style. Drop it straight down and jig it, pull it along the bottom, experiment until you find what's working.

CHAPTER 3

Trout & Salmon

114. Where Trout Are Always Hungry

Small streams that flow into some of the best wilderness streams don't have the amounts of food and insect life of the large rivers. The water is swift, and the trout will quickly grab prey floating into view. Some anglers mistakenly think these trout are stupid, but they're not. They're just hungry. Use floating flies like Royal Coachmen, Stimulators, and Humpies.

115. Make Your Dropper Fly Expendable

When tying a dropper leader to a dry fly or strike indicator, make the dropper in a lighter strength than your main leader. When you hit a snag, you're better off losing the dropper fly instead of your whole rig.

116. The Dry Fly As a Striker Indicator

Whether your dry fly is one to search the water, or one to match a specific hatch, make sure it's large enough, and buoyant enough, to give your dropper leader and nymph a good floating

platform, visible throughout its drift. If your dry fly is too small, or your nymph too large and heavy, you'll defeat your entire purpose.

117. Where Are the Hatches?

Among the lessons about trout fishing that have cost me considerable gobs of both time and money, one of the most important has been the realization that even on those rare days when hatches occur, they do not happen everywhere. Don't expect the entire surface of the river to burst with emerging caddis and mayflies. Hatches occur—*when* they occur—in scattered sections of the river, in varying water types. A riffle, a smooth glide, a deep pool—all might harbor hatches at different and varying times. You might have great fishing in hatches at one small section of the river at dusk, then meet your buddy at the truck later and learn that he saw nothing—no rises. Big rivers or small streams, that's the way it goes.

118. Upstream with Dries, Downstream Nymphs and Streamers

Stu Apte loves trout fishing almost as much as he does fishing for tarpon and bonefish. His favorite strategy is to fish part of a big river or small stream upstream with dry flies, then take a break and rig for nymphs and streamers and fish back downstream. This system can be particularly effective when you're fishing dries early in the morning, then switching to nymphs and heading back downstream as the sun gets overhead.

119. Small Stream, Small Backpack, Big Day

Do everything you possibly can to find a small trout stream tucked away among the hills and mountains—the Appalachians, the Rocky Mountain high country, the New England ranges, the midwest forests, the northwest peaks. Once you find a stream that's just right, lots of clean water and trout (most of them won't be big, but so what?), completely isolated, enjoy it to the hilt as often as you can by strapping on a small backpack that has everything you need for a full day's fishing, pick up your light rod, and go. If you've never done this, I hope you give it a try. Someday you'll thank me!

120. Give Small-Stream Trout Your Best Shot

Fish small trout streams slowly and carefully in an upstream direction. Keep your casts short, popping your fly into tiny pockets. Short, accurate casts are everything.

121. Finding and Fishing the Seams

Seams are places in the river current where a slight change-of-pace in the flow occurs between fast water and slow water. Imagine a rock in the stream. Think of the water rushing past on both sides as the fast lanes. The slow or still water behind the rock and directly in front are the slow lanes. Between the fast and slow lanes will be seams of intermediate flow, perfect for trout to ambush prey.

122. Spring Creeks: Superb Trout Destinations

Flowing up clean and cold from aquifers and chalk beds inside Mother Earth, twenty-four hours a day, seven days a week, 365 days a year, spring creeks are worth every hour and every cent trout addicts spend to find and fish them. Here are trout you can *see,* prolific insect hatches, and easier wading than the rough-and-tumble freestone streams. They are tough to fish, but . . . so what? You can find plenty of them in Pennsylvania, scattered throughout the upper Midwest and far West, and in England the chalk streams are angling destinations to die for.

123. When You Can't Match the Hatch

One of the most frustrating experiences in trout fishing is to find yourself in the midst of a big hatch of insects, with trout taking them eagerly, and you just can't seem to get the right fly onto them. This happens all the time with hatches like the tiny Tricos. Instead of letting frustration overwhelm you, try putting on a fly that totally changes the pace of what's going on. Use a No. 16 Royal Wulff or Fan-Winged Royal Coachman, for instance, or a buggy terrestrial imitation. And there's always room for the Adams, the go-to fly when nothing else is working. The Stimulator ranks high with go-to flies also.

124. When Rain Is Your Friend

No one especially likes fishing in the rain—and thunderstorms are downright dangerous—but there are times when rain comes in just the right amounts at the right time to get trout moving and feeding. The rain washes all kinds of terrestrials and morsels into the stream, and the trout go after them with vigor. The only way you'll find out if it's a "good rain" or "bad rain" is to be out there. Chances are you'll have the stream to yourself. And, whatever you do, don't miss the spots where other streams or runs pour into the main river.

125. Where the Road Leaves the River

Some fishing tips seem so simple—like sharpening your hooks—that most people probably ignore them. A simple one that I hope you will not ignore is this: Fish where the road leaves the river. Walk to where the crowds don't go, and you will be rewarded with better trout fishing. Most people will not walk there. They just won't do it. At a health club I sometimes go to for workouts, I watch in fascination as people maneuver and jostle their cars into parking positions close to the front door. All that so they don't have to walk a couple hundred feet across a big parking lot. Walking . . . to do the very thing they came to the club for, getting exercise. It makes no sense. Neither does not walking into the woods to fish where you can't see the road. But that's what people do.

126. Sulphurs: The Year's Best Fly Hatch

In the West they have the glorious Pale Morning Dun hatches that fill the air with greenish-yellow bugs. In the East and upper Midwest, the highlight of the springtime hatches sees the arrival of a similar mayfly—the Sulphurs, most in the genus *Ephemerella* in various sizes with other Latin subtitles for those who take their fishing and fly-tying with textbook correctness. Where I fish, mostly in Pennsylvania and New Jersey, the hatches begin in mid-May, a week or so after the storied Hendricksons have played out. The party goes on until late in June, with the fishing getting tougher as it progresses.

127. Barbless Hooks Make More Sense

Required in many trout streams, barbless hooks have a lot going for them in every form of light-tackle fishing, fresh and salt water. First, they are easy to extract when the angler sinks one into his hand or body. Second, they are easier to extract from the fish, allowing your catch to be released and live to fight another day. Finally, they sink deeper than barbed hooks, making most hook-ups just as effective as barbed hooks.

128. Wading Staffs Make Sense

Falling down while wading and fishing isn't fun—on any kind of water, small creeks or big rivers. You'll get hurt, break or lose some tackle, or at least get wet, possibly very wet. Small streams have rocks, slippery and rounded. Large rivers have powerful current, and sometimes, as a bonus, slippery and rounded rocks. If you're a geezer, you already know darn well you need a wading staff. If you're coming onto geezer age, you're probably thinking about using one. If you're young and strong, you probably think wading staffs are for geezers only. Wading staffs, clipped to your fly vest, whether homemade or store bought, make life so easy. If your legs are in the least unsteady, try using one. You'll never go wade fishing again without it.

129. Netting Your Trout

Making wild swipes at the water with your net is a sure way to knock a trout—big or small—off the line. Jabbing at the fish tail-first is another bad move. The right way: Submerge your net, pull the fish over it headfirst, and lift. You've got him!

130. When Summer Trout Move Out

During extremely hot weather, the real dog days of summer, you may not find trout bunched at the mouths of spring creeks entering your river. Look for them up the creek itself. They'll be very spooky, but they'll be there. Realize that many trout anglers do not fish during times like this, when the fish are under stress.

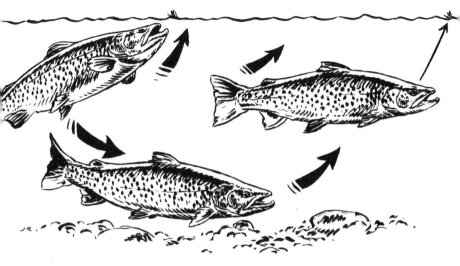

131. Where Trout Hold and Where They Rise

When trout are in holding water, they fin slowly, suspended, facing into the current. When they rise to take a fly, the splash or tiny swirl you see will usually be a little downstream of their holding lie. They take the fly, then swim back into their holding position. Keep that in mind when targeting your cast.

132. Fish Big Boulders on Both Sides

As soon as most trout anglers take up the sport, they learn to expect trout to be lying in the pockets behind boulders. The front sides of boulders also contain pockets, and the trout love them.

133. You Have to Be Sneaky to Catch Trout

Your approach to trout stream pools, and your very first casts, mean everything to your ultimate success. Careless approaches and careless casts will spook trout, sending them bolting from the pool, or—and this happens more often—alert trout that

Roll Cast

something is amiss. Once alerted, they may not strike for some time. You'll be thinking, "They're not biting today." But that's not the case at all.

134. The Roll Cast: A Fly-Fishing Must

Not only is the Roll Cast useful for freeing your fly from snags, in many situations you will not have room behind you or to the side for a backcast. That's where the Roll Cast will pay big dividends for every moment you've spent learning it.

135. The Dry Fly Fished Downstream on Big Rivers

Although upstream stalking and casting is the tradition for dry fly fishing, many shrewd anglers who fish big-water rivers like the Delaware in the East and the upper Missouri in the West favor a downstream cast. They get into position a good distance above

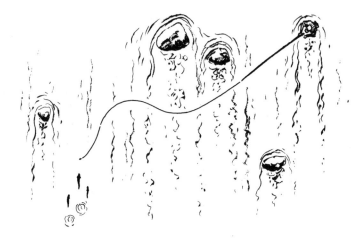

the fish and slightly to the side. They cast quartering downstream to the rising fish, then mend the line upstream to get a straight downstream line-leader-fly float—without drag.

136. Ripping Streamers

Sometimes the only way to get into position to work streamers through likely looking water is from the downstream side, casting upstream. Then you have to remember that your fly is floating toward you very swiftly with the current. To get any realistic movement at all on the fly, you need to be retrieving line so fast that the act has come to be called "ripping streamers" by many fly fishers.

137. And Still Champion: The Muddler Minnow

The Muddler Minnow has probably made more "Best Fly" lists than any other. Why? Because it catches trout. You can find it in every fly shop and fly-fishing catalog, in many hook sizes. You can dress it and fish it dry on the surface; you can work it down and across like a streamer; and you can let it bounce along the bottom like a nymph. Like the Woolly Bugger, the Muddler Minnow belongs in your fly box.

138. Nymph Fishing Made Easy

The greatest discovery in the history of fly fishing—as far as float-fishing guides in the high-country West have discovered—is nymph fishing. Not the classic nymph fishing of most American trout streams, spawned from English experts like Frank

Sawyer and company, but using a couple of nymphs tied in tandem below a strike indicator that floats on the surface. That strike indicator—they come in all different shapes and sizes—is nothing more than an elaborate bobber. Picture this: You started out years and years ago fishing with a bobber. Now, you've got the money and time to book a top guide on one of Montana's top streams, like the Big Horn or Beaverhead, and you're floating along in the raft chunking out a stretch of fly line (yes, "chunking" is the right word, not "casting") with a couple of weighted nymphs tied to a "bobber"—aka, "strike indicator"—riding the current. Okay, you're having fun, catching trout. I have no problem with that, so long as you see the irony.

139. Trout Under the Bridge

"Any fisherman with more than a morning's experience knows that the water beneath a bridge is a likely lie for a trout; and often,

for a big trout. It is that rare phenomenon, the 'complete' lie . . .
The narrower a section of the river is, the deeper it will be . . . "
—John Goddard and Brian Clarke, *Understanding Trout
Behavior*, 2001

140. The Perfect Small-Stream Trout Rod

Opinions abound on the subject of the perfect rod for small-
stream trout fishing. Here's one you can take to the bank: You
want a short rod, 7 feet, to handle the overhanging limbs and
close brush along the sides of the stream. You must have a fast,
powerful tip. It will get your short line out fast and sure. You

want all this in the lightest rod you can find, one that comes alive in your hand. You'll enjoy every cast, and the feel of a fighting fish will be your ultimate reward. The long-rod advocates will cry "Foul!" at this opinion, claiming to have more control with the longer stick. To each his own. In small streams, go with the short rod and keep your fly and line in the water instead of the trees and bushes.

141. Guaranteed: More Trout Spinning Small Streams

Dunking worms in deep holes for early-season trout in your favorite stream is relatively easy—as long as other anglers don't take over your hole. Spinning the entire stream, working your way carefully from pocket to pocket, is a lot more fun and will produce lots of trout, provided you are a skilled caster. The ability to cast light spinners and baits into pockets with accuracy separates the trout anglers who limit-out from the ones who come up empty. They just can't cast. We're talking about all kinds of delicate casts, underhand flips, sidearm throws under brush, things like that. It's not distance; it's accuracy that counts. The only way to obtain this skill is to practice, practice, practice. You'll catch lots of trout if you do.

142. Best Bait for Early-Season Spinning

Hitting your favorite local trout stream when it's stocked with fish in early season is a coveted rite of spring. An absolutely deadly bait—even better than worms—is the mealworm, the larva form of the mealworm beetle. Find a baitshop that carries them, and you are in business. You can also order them live right off the internet at places like Cabelas, www.cabelas.com. (They'll keep in your frig.) Place a No. 6 or 8 bait hook about three-fourths of the length of the beetle. Notice that stuff will be oozing out of the beetle, creating a fantastic fish attractor. Use a single split-shot to get the bait down. Many anglers like a barrel swivel about 18 inches above the hook to prevent twists. Mealies stay on the hook fairly well. Cast them into pocket water, in front of boulders, around their sides, into deep holes, down through riffles. Using ultralight spinning gear, mealies, and a rig like this, you're going to catch lots of early-season trout.

143. Small Spinners for Small-Stream Trout

If you are a good caster, you can do very well on early season trout in small streams by using ultralight spinning tackle and the smallest, lightest in-line spinners your rig can handle. Mepps, Panther Martin, and Blue Fox are some favorites, but there are many others. The bigger and heavier the spinner, the bigger and deeper the water it takes to fish them without them hanging up constantly. You want the lightest spinners your stream can handle, working them into pockets and under overhanging cover. Casting and retrieving these spinners in a small stream is an art unto itself, as challenging as fly fishing—but a lot more productive most of the time.

144. The Downstream Swing: Your Spinner's Strike Zone

When your spinner is swinging on the downstream arc of your cast, just before it swings across the current and the line straightens out below you, don't be in a hurry. Far from it, realize that the next several seconds may bring the strike you've been waiting for. Alternate between little jerks and steady pulls as it swings across. When it's downstream directly below you, keep it still for a moment, then start a careful retrieve.

145. Small-Stream Spinning: The Real Art

The real magicians of small-stream spinning—the guys and gals who catch most of the trout—avoid snagging by careful

manipulation of their line with a subtle sense of feel in their rod hand. They don't make long casts; you might even say they don't cast at all in the true sense of the word. Instead, they make little flips and tosses, putting the small spinner into the holes with backhand and sidearm moves. They also match the size and weight of the spinner to the conditions, and often hold their rod high on the retrieve to keep the lure from snagging the bottom. A good formula to remember: Flip the spinner out rod-low and retrieve it rod-high, watching the line carefully to make sure your little Mepps isn't about to snag up.

146. Fish the Woolly Bugger with Spinning Tackle

Tie on an olive Woolly Bugger streamer, place enough split-shot to make the cast about 8 inches up the line, and fish it just as if you were using a fly rod. Whether or not to use a weighted bead-head fly, or the unweighted, depends on the current and depth you're trying to fish. Olive Woolly Buggers in various weights and sizes belong in your kit with your Mepps and other in-line spinners.

147. Fishing the Big, Slow Pools

When you're lucky enough to get a big slow pool all to yourself on your trout stream, don't make your first casts to the backside. Start by making a series of Fan Casts to the nearest part of the pool, gradually working your casts to the backside. You'll really be covering the water that way.

148. Matukas and Spinners: A Deadly Combo

A Web site called Jerry's Flies, www.jerrysflies.com, is where I first started reading about Matuka spinner flies. Combining a Matuka streamer with a spinner creates a lure you can count on to get trout moving in whatever pool you work it in. Matukas, which I believe originally came from New Zealand, have been a favorite of trout fly fishers for years. Combined with a spinner, they are even more effective. Before Woolly Buggers came along, the Matuka was my go-to fly for searching the water. I like olive.

149. Spinning Tricks for Trout

You don't hear much about "spinning the bubble" these days, but it's still an effective way to catch trout on streams or lakes where all-tackle fishing is allowed. Tie your spinning line to the kind of ball float that you can get water into to add weight for casting with flies. Set your leader from the float to the depth you think will bring strikes, and tie on a nymph. Cast upstream, downstream, or across and let your rig float down through trout lairs. You'll catch fish.

150. Pool Etiquette: It Makes Sense

There are violations all over the map, but *there is* a correct way to share the fishing in a steelhead or salmon pool where several anglers are gathered. Starting at the top of the pool, make a cast that allows your fly to swing down and across the hotspot or strike zone. Next take a step downstream and make another cast. Keep repeating the steps and casts until you reach the bottom of the pool, then go back to the top and start over. Of course, this assumes you are fishing with considerate sportsmen and women. You will on occasion run across a complete jerk and idiot who wants to camp on the best water and keep it for himself. When that happens, it's time for a diplomatic conversation.

151. The Truth About Atlantic Salmon Fishing

My friend Jim Merritt, one of the finest anglers I know and author of many articles on the subject, raises an interesting point about Atlantic salmon fishing: "With about a zillion books on trout fishing tactics, why are there only a few on Atlantic salmon fishing tactics? Is it not because fly fishing for salmon—both Atlantic and Pacific types—basically consists of making a cast quartering upstream and then letting your fly swing down and across? You might put a few mends in your line, straightening it out or

getting a deeper drift and swing, but basically that's it. Cast after cast." Jim's dead right.

152. How to Get More Salmon Strikes

Leonard M. Wright, Jr., was a keen student of all forms of fly fishing for trout and salmon, with vast experience in fishing for both. From his Atlantic salmon experiences, he became convinced that most salmon casts resulted in the fly passing over and past the fish, too shallow and too fast. The speed and depth of the fly became critical issues to Wright, and he went to a method of fishing his salmon flies "low and slow." Wright says, "Many times I have heard salmon anglers claim that . . . the most killing part of any presentation occurs during the last part of the swing when the fly is straightening out below them." Wright became convinced that the catch success when the fly "is straightening out below them" was due to the speed having been too fast in the earlier parts of the presentation. Only in the last critical moments was the speed of the fly right for the salmon to take a look.

153. Current Seams: Where the Trout Are

"Then consider a trout's other requirements in moving water—relief from the current and shelter from danger—and you'll know where to begin. Target the edges of eddies, slower-water seams, and deep runs that are close to the main current. Trout swim out, take a food item, and return to cover."

—Dick Galland, "Master Basic Nymphing,"
in *Fly Fisherman* magazine's
"Nymphing for Trout" booklet

154. The Hardest Fish to Predict

Everybody knows that in Atlantic salmon fishing, even after months of planning and dreaming, you might arrive at your river and find: 1) The fish aren't in yet. They're still holding offshore, waiting for the right water levels and temperature; 2) The fish have come and gone; 3) The water is high, and staying high, and the fish are running the river, not staying in pools; or 4) The water is low, hot, and the fish are dour, holding in some pools but taking absolutely nothing. In this instance, it may start to rain on your final day in camp, and when you return home you'll be subjected to the phone call that exalts, "Just after you left . . . "

155. Why Salmon Hit Flies

It's an old, old argument, with opinions from all sides, so I might as well weigh in with my own. The question before the House is: "Since they are not feeding when they enter rivers to spawn, why do salmon hit flies?" Experts of every stripe have discussed the subject, in print, and I must side with Lee Wulff in believing that salmon take the fly due to a flash of memory from their years in the river as a parr. When certain conditions are absolutely right—the speed of the fly in the water, the slant of light on the fly's colors, the temperature—a salmon urged by some inner biological need to be "on the take" will hit a fly.

156. A Salmon Remembers

When Atlantic salmon fishing, one often hooks and reels in tiny parr that have eagerly attacked the fly. Years later, when the salmon returns from the ocean depths to its home river, memories of its years chasing flies will be strong enough to cause a response to your bogus fly if . . . and it's a big IF . . . the bite is on and conditions are right. A "taking fish" can be hard to find.

157. Hook a Salmon, Break a Rod

Alaskan guides have told me that they probably see more rods broken by chum salmon than any other types. The chums come in just before, and with, the silvers, and they can be big—topping 20 pounds. Add mint condition, fresh from the salt, and you've got a fish that will take you deep, deep into the backing. When trying to "horse" such a big fish in the final stages of the fight, many anglers over-stress the rod by pulling back hard just as the fish launches a final desperate run.

158. When the Bite Is On

When fishing for Atlantic or Pacific salmon there are certain times when the fish are in a taking mode, "on the bite," as anglers love to say. When this happens, for whatever reason—barometer, temperature, light, moon phases, whatever—have your line in the water and keep fishing hard. It won't last!

159. When Salmon Strike

The strike of the Atlantic salmon is one of fly fishing's most treasured moments. Alas, it can be a short-lived moment if you react too quickly and pull the fly away from the fish. If your nerves are steady enough, the salmon will usually hook itself. Raise the rod slowly, feel the line tighten, and get set for a battle royal. Many salmon are hooked during idle moments when the angler is looking away or talking to a companion. A hair-trigger reaction to a strike is not the way to go.

160. Buck Or Roe? You'll Feel the Difference

The male shad, the buck, leaps more and makes flashy runs. The roe, the female laden with eggs, the one you're after, makes your rod and line feel as if perhaps you've hooked the bottom. Then the "bottom" begins moving and pulling hard and steady, and you know you're in for a fight.

161. Same Spot, Same Lures, Different Results

When you see two boats working on a shad holding pool or run, slinging shad darts, and one boat is taking fish while the other is getting casting practice, you can bet heavy money the losers are not fishing deep enough. If your dart is not heavy enough, you won't get down to the fish.

CHAPTER 4

Walleye

162. White-Water Walleye Holes

In summer when walleyes go deep and may be tough to find in schools on the reefs, the current below the rapids on lake outlets can usually be counted on to give up some fish. They have everything they need here: plenty of oxygen, food coming their way, and cover to hide.

163. Walleyes for the Frying Pan: Beware the Cholesterol Police

You will not find many anglers who don't rank the walleye as No. 1 in the frying pan. For my taste, the fillets should be fried, even deep-fried. Yes, the docs will call this a heart-stopping meal, and that might keep you away. But . . . what the heck. How often do

you do it? Some of the best meals I've ever had in my life have been shoreline lunches with walleye and pike fillets fried in a pan that the guides had first used to fry great slices of bacon as soon as they got the fire going. The Cholesterol Police were shouting in my ear, but I dug in with great gusto. Life's too short to miss this kind of culinary experience.

164. Live-Bait Rig for Taking More Walleyes

A simple rig to catch more and bigger walleyes is to use a slip-sinker system, with a sliding egg or bullet sinker in front of a barrel swivel, with a leader that varies from 6 to 10 feet.

CHAPTER 5

Panfish, Catfish & Carp

165. Springtime Fun Guaranteed

For a mixed-bag springtime catch of crappies, bluegills, perch, walleyes, bass—you name it—fish a small jig, sweetened with a minnow hooked upwards through the lip, and use a sliding bobber at your preferred depth. Experiment to find the depth where you're getting strikes and enjoying the pulls and fun that make you feel like a kid again. Use ¼-, ⅛-, or ¹⁄₁₆-ounce jigheads, with white or yellow soft-plastic grubs, such as Kalin's Triple Threat (Bass Pro Shops). Your preferred float, stick, or bobber, should be on the small side to be sensitive to tentative cold-water hits.

166. Watch Those Spinner Blades

That spinners for panfish need to be small is fairly basic know-how, but often overlooked is the need for the spinner blades to be thin, therefore turning easily and quickly at the slightest and slowest pull.

167. Which Crappie Is That?

Because the crappie is such a popular and widespread fish—famous for both the action and in the pan—much confusion exists over crappie identification. White crappie, black crappie, calico bass—three names, but, whoops, there are only two fish, two real crappies. The white crappie is the most common and widely distributed. The black crappie is the fish sometimes called "calico bass," although at times you will also hear the white crappie called "calico bass." It's very confusing, but throw out the "calico" label and you have the two fish everybody catches and loves to eat—white crappie and black crappie. The dorsal fins of both fish are different, but the easiest way to distinguish between the white and black crappie is by noting that the spots on the white crappie are arranged in neat vertical bars, while on the black crappie they are scattered randomly along the sides of the fish.

168. Fly-Fishing Bonus: Bluegills on the Bed

When bluegills are bedding—the time varies greatly from area to area—fly fishing for these hard-fighting panfish really comes into its own. After you spot the smoothed, rounded patches of the spawning beds, cast a nymph on a light leader into the spots and let it sink onto the beds. A bluegill will pick it up, take it off the bed, and then spit it out. The fish are not feeding, only housekeeping.

169. Don't Lose That Fish

They don't call crappies "papermouths" for nothing. Those lips with the wide section of thin membrane mean that you can never be sure of a fish until it's in the boat. Crappies, even big ones, are not powerful fighters, but what they lack in power they make up for in suspense, since your hook can pull loose at any moment. I've seen some crappies-to-die-for lost right at the net or hand when the hook broke through the lips of the "paper mouth."

170. Catching Slab-Sided Bluegills in Midsummer

In the heat and blazing suns of high summer, you probably won't have much luck catching the really big bluegills by fishing your usual spots—shoreline cover, stumps, fallen trees. The occasional good fish might be taken early or late in the day, but mostly the pickings will be slim. Still, provided your lake has a healthy bluegill population, the slab-sided fish you covet can be found and taken. Instead of target casting to cover, fish for them deep with 1/16- or 1/32-ounce jigs, straight over the sides of the boat. Yes, straight down! Slowly work the jigs up and down at various depths and locations until you find the fish. Note the level where you've finally hit the schools of big fish, and you'll be in business of a close-up of the fish with the jig in the corner of its mouth.

171. Go Deep With Sponge-Rubber Spiders

Those sponge-rubber spiders that look and feel real enough to bite you will catch far, far bigger bluegills if you wrap some lead wire around their heads. They're made to be fished on top, but that's seldom where the big 'gills are hanging out. They're deep. You've got to find them, then get your spider down to them.

172. Catching Big, Summer Yellow Perch

Yellow perch are prime targets for anglers everywhere, but especially in the Great Lakes region where they grow big and fat. Veteran angler Steve Ryan explains how to cash in on the action in the article "Summer Perchin'" on the Lindy Tackle Web site, www.lindyfishingtackle.com: "Lake Michigan's fishery has changed considerably over the last several decades but the methods for catching these tasty fish remain the same. Crappie spreaders, Lindy rigs, jigs, and slip floats will catch you a limit of perch no matter where you fish. These rigs are nothing more than bait delivery systems designed to present live bait to fish in the most effective means possible." Ryan likes to set up his rigs with minnows when the water is cold, then night crawlers or softshell crawfish when the water temperatures top the mid-50s. See his article for more details.

173. Try Crankbaits for Summer Crappies

If you're not happy with the numbers of crappies you've been getting in summer, try using crankbaits. Especially on larger waters, where the crappie schools roam around a lot, and where they often go deep, crankbaits either cast or trolled can produce big crappies for you. Some favorite models of top guides include the 2-inch Bandits in sizes that dive to varying depths, and Rebel's 2-inch Deep Vee-R, which dives to 8 to 10 feet.

174. Where to Find Redbreast

Redbreasts live and thrive in clean, dark, low-country currents of the southeastern United States that sweep over sandy bottoms, glaring white when the sun hits them, and through boggy swamplands of oaks, cypress, sweet gums, and magnolia. Towering pines loom on the higher ground along the serpentine courses of the rivers and creeks, where the never-ending cries of birds mark the flow.

175. Count on the Catalpa Worm

If you're fortunate enough to live in the South, treasure every catalpa tree you can find. For the catalpa caterpillar is the ultimate live bait for bluegills, redbreasts, and just about every other fish swimming in southern waters. Some of the old-timers used to recommend turning the catalpa insideout. Experiment if you wish, but I don't think you have to. Catalpa bonus: You can keep them in the fridge.

176. Cricket Know-How

Crickets are a mainstay of panfishing with live bait—and a mainstay of bait shops—but they come off the hook easily and you'll be plagued by minnows and tiny fish constantly stealing your bait. They're best used when you're after *big* panfish.

177. Giant Catfish: You Need Help

The biggest catfish—we're talking 20 to 30 pounds and higher— are caught on the bigger rivers, from deep holes. Fishing these waters, particularly where impoundment water is being released, can be treacherous. Think about hiring a guide before you tackle it on your own.

178. Favorite Baits for Blue Cats

"For whopper blues, stick to fish. Big catfish almost exclusively eat other fish. Use whole fish, 4- to 6-inch-long strips or meaty chunks," reports John M. Felsher in "Big Game Sport on a Small Budget," on a www.cabelas.com Field Guide Story. Some of the largest blues hit "mere morsels," he says. Felsher notes that some guides prefer skipjack herring, cut into chunks or filleted. The fillet is hooked one time with the hook exposed and undulates in the current. Catfish can't resist it.

179. Best Water for Small-Stream Catfish

"Most people think catfish hang in deep, quiet holes. This may be true of the bigger ones, but smaller cats feed in shallow, swift areas. I'm talking about runs that are 2–3 feet deep and exposed to direct current. Also, a spot is better if it has a clean gravel or clay bottom instead of a mud bottom. Catfish hold around cover (logs, treetops, rocks, and so on) in these areas and move out into the current to find food. In fact, they feed a lot like a bass."

—Buffalo River, Tennessee angler Joe B. Sweeney, in the Wade Bourne article "Lazy Days: Small Streams and Southern Catfish," Bass Pro Shops Outdoor Library

180. Don't Forget Carp Fishing

They're big and powerful, capable of making your reel sing and putting a bend in your rod that seems dangerously close to breaking. Although not one of the glamour girls and boys of fishing—and not good to eat (for most of us, anyway)—carp are a worthy gamefish that will pay you back in fun for every hour you put into learning how to catch them. In England, carp fishing has a fanatical army of devotees. We have our share of carp addicts here as well, and once you've tried the sport, you may find yourself hooked.

181. To Catch Carp, Pass the Dough

You'll hear it from every side: Dough makes a wonderful bait to catch those bottom-feeding carp. Your first thought may be, "How the heck do I keep dough balls on a hook?" Major hook manufacturers such as Eagle Claw and Mustad have the specialized treble hooks carp anglers need to fish dough balls and other creative baits. A common rig is to use a sinker at the end of the line with two 12-inch dropper lines about a foot or two apart above. Carp have no teeth, so special leaders are not needed.

182. Essentials for Catching More Carp

Although they are not good on the table, carp are plentiful, powerful, and are best caught on lighter tackle than many other sportfish. You'll catch more carp by using a hook that is not too big—certainly no bigger than a 1/0 max—and a small split-shot sinker, or no sinker at all. Carp will not pick up bait and take it if they feel any resistance. Dough balls, corn, and other homemade concoctions make the best baits. See Cabelas and others for special hooks and tackle.

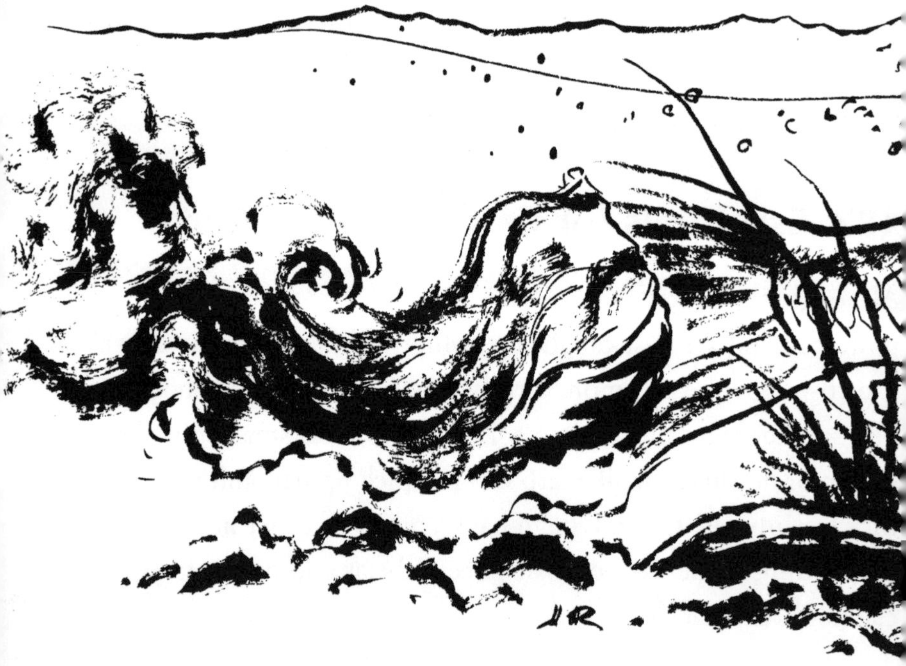

CHAPTER 6

Pickerel, Pike & Muskie

183. On the Hunt for Pike

Northern pike, and their smaller cousins, chain pickerel, are masters of the art of ambush—fierce predators roaming the water in wolf packs. They're not always around, and sometimes they don't seem to be on the bite, but if you're fishing good pike or pickerel water, you should be in for prime action. Weedy, still-water bays with deeper "escape" water nearby are where you should find the fish.

184. A Fish of Wildness

Pike are similar to brook trout and lake trout in that their prime environment is the great north country. If you haven't been there, you owe it to yourself to do everything you can to plan such a trip. From Minnesota's Boundary Waters Area and the adjoining Quetico, up through all the vast reaches of the Canadian wilderness, wolf packs of pike patrol through the cold, clean waters.

This is the land of spruce, white pine, and birch; of loons calling from across the lakes; of beavers, otters, and mink; of moose and black bear. If your heart cranks up a notch or two when you think about country like this, and the fish that swim there, you'll know you've just got to go.

185. Playing Those Pike

Despite their great size and fierce disposition, northern pike sometimes seem on the sluggish side when you're playing them. Then it happens: The pike sees the boat. It's a whole new ball-game now; time to hold on to your hat. The pike will pull the trigger, your rod will bow into a hoop, and you'll know you're in a fight.

186. The Perfect Pike Spoon or Spinner

The perfect pike spoon or spinner is the one that will wobble, flash, and give the most action at the *slowest* retrieving speed.

CHAPTER 7

Saltwater Fish

187. The Saltwater Challenge

The rivers that drain into the ocean, the bays that receive them, and the great seas beyond can be heaven for anglers. However, their sheer size makes them a formidable challenge for anglers whose

only experience has been in fresh water. When my father, brother, and I began fishing the Chesapeake Bay in the mid-1950s, we had a 19-foot Whirlwind boat, but virtually no knowledge of exactly how and where to use it from its dock in Annapolis. Thus began a learning process that took some years. Talking with other anglers, tackle and boat shop keepers, taking charter trips—all these activities were necessary parts of the famous School of Hard Knocks. I would not trade the experience for anything, and would do it all over again. But, unless you come from a family of saltwater anglers—or have been under the wing of a friendly neighbor who fishes the salt (and perhaps has a boat!)—be prepared to ask questions, read a lot, check the Internet a lot, take charter trips whenever you can, and experiment on your own to learn your way in fishing the big waters at the edge of the sea.

188. Head Boats Can Be Great Fun

Those fishing boats where you pay your way onto a boat right at the dock—they're called head boats—can be great fun, especially if it's your only way to get saltwater action or you're new and learning. Anywhere within a couple of hours driving distance to the salt, the Thursday and Friday newspapers will have ads and fishing reports for the popular boats leaving for blues, stripers, flounder, blackfish, porgies—whatever's running. Some trips are for the day, some half-days. Take your lunch and snacks in a small cool. The boats have the gear and the mates to show you how to use it. There are big-fish pools for fun and winning a few bucks if you're lucky. You can have a great day out there, and it's a great place to take kids.

189. The Bluefish Frenzy: You've Got to Be There

Whether you are out for the pan-sized blues called "snappers" in bays and coves, or the 15- to 20-plus pounders called "slammers" just offshore, you're in for rod-bending, tackle-busting action like few fishing trips can provide. And despite the complaints of those who don't like to eat them, many of us bluefish addicts think they're great on the table, especially when freshly caught. Even if you live in Kansas or Iowa, put bluefishing on your list of Things To Do Before You Die. By the way, if you're a trout fisherman and thinking of taking that small reel along, forget about it! A bluefish will blow it to pieces in one run.

190. Chumming: The Saltwater Action Creator

When you experience chumming for saltwater gamefish on charter trips or with friends who are showing you the way, you'll quickly learn to appreciate this fun and deadly way of fishing. Anchored in a likely spot for waves of moving fish or over a mother lode of suspended fish which are happy to not be going anywhere, you'll be grinding and chopping small baitfish, clams, and other delicacies and feeding the gump into the tides. Once a long "slick" is established, work your jigs or baited hooks into the "hot zone" and hang onto your hat. Chumming is saltwater's light-tackle heaven.

191. When the Blues Are Running

"A school of blues can send panic hundreds of yards forward of their path as they wheel and turn en masse on feeding forays, making terror-stricken baitfish jump through the water's surface like a volley of arrows . . . He is a fierce predator, savagely running down and chewing up anything in his path—including other blues."

—Stephen Ferber, *Sports Afield Fishing Annual*

192. An Extra Bluefish Danger

When landing bluefish, "The one constant danger lies in the lure itself. Remember, there are nine hooks in each plug. The chopper jumps, twists, shakes, and thrashes after he's brought over the side. In many occasions, you'll have more than one hooked blue in the boat at the same time—so getting one of those barbs through the finger is a real possibility even for the most experienced of men."

—Stephen Ferber, *Sports Afield Fishing Annual*

193. Great Autumn Surf Fishing

In October and November along the Atlantic coast, reports J.B. Kasper in his *Trenton Times* outdoor column, storms push a lot of clams into the wash along the beaches, making them the bait of choice the first few days after a big blow. Kasper says to look for

some of the best movements of stripers and blues, " . . . just after the new and full moon, especially when the top of the tide occurs around sundown and sunset."

194. When the Mackerel Run

When the mackerel tide flows north along the Atlantic coastline every spring, and anglers enjoy the year's first big run of fish, many of the mackerel-fishing faithful do not realize that these little torpedo-like speedsters are part of a great tribe of saltwater battlers, including tuna, marlin, and sailfish. The mackerel is also related to the albacores, bonitos, giant kingfish, wahoo, and the Spanish and cerro mackerels. The mackerel is the smallest of all his relatives, but anglers don't mind a bit when the action begins.

195. Surf Fishing's Scouting Report

Next to seeing fish breaking and knowing exactly where the action is (instead of guessing where it might eventually happen), try to get a look at your stretch of beach at extreme low tides. Study where even the smallest cuts and channels show on the bottom. That's where you're likely to get strikes when the waves move in, bringing the fish with them on a rising tide.

196. The Joys of Full-Moon Fishing

When you're on the beach for stripers and blues when the moon is full, or nearly full, and the skies are reasonably clear of clouds, you'll enjoy night fishing with almost-daylight visibility.

197. Heed the Call of the Surf

If the call of the surf—the breaking waves, the flowing tides, the onshore and offshore birds with their flights and cries, the great vastness of sky and salt-scented air—means anything at all to you, I'd like to give you a shove, not a nudge, toward getting into surf fishing. In autumn, in particular, when the crowds have mostly gone and the fish are at their best, on the move, the great

surf-fishing beaches like those in New Jersey can provide magi-
cal angling days. With your daypack—food and beverage, even
something to read if you like—and your tackle, you're all set. The
very best way to get into it is to hire a guide a couple of times,
let him show you the gear, the techniques that work best—before
you blow a lot of money on the wrong stuff. There are also many
clubs and associations, or perhaps you have a friend who can show
you the ropes and tools. Most of the people who are really crazy
about surf fishing have found they don't have to catch a lot of fish
to have a good day on the beach. Of course, catching fish is what
really makes surf fishing exciting. Just beachcombing won't cut it.

133

198. Lefty Kreh's "Miracle" Saltwater Fly

"Lefty's Deceiver is now used around the world in salt water (although it is a popular freshwater pattern as well). Without being boastful, I think it's accurate to say that the Deceiver and the old Clouser Minnow are two of the most imitated saltwater flies in the sport." [Editor's Note: Lefty Kreh's Deceiver was honored by the United States Postal Service in 1991 by being chosen to illustrate a 29-cent postage stamp. Lefty says he is very proud that the caption doesn't read, "Deceiver," but instead reads, "Lefty's Deceiver."]

—Lefty Kreh, with Chris Millard, *My Life Was THIS BIG and Other True Fishing Tales,* Skyhorse Publishing, 2008

199. The Standard Fly Casting Method Doesn't Work

"In the standard method the angler basically brings the rod from 10 o'clock back to about 2 o'clock and then back to 10 o'clock. After trying the technique for a while I began to realize that it was not the best, most efficient way to cast a fly line."

—Lefty Kreh, with Chris Millard, *My Life Was THIS BIG and Other True Fishing Tales,* Skyhorse Publishing, 2008

200. The Lefty Kreh Fly Casting Technique

"Through trial and error I gradually learned to take the rod way back behind me and make longer backcasts and longer forward casts. I also abandoned the high-hand vertical style of the standard method and adopted a much lower position, a more horizontal profile for my arm. As I began to refine my technique I found that I was not only making longer, more accurate casts with tighter loops, but I was doing it with far less effort than the old 10 to 2 method demanded."

—Lefty Kreh, with Chris Millard, *My Life Was THIS BIG and Other True Fishing Tales,* Skyhorse Publishing, 2008

201. Lefty Kreh's Fly Casting Revolution

"In March 1965, I wrote an article detailing my new technique in *Outdoor Life.* Many people view that article as a landmark in the evolution of the fly cast. To this day, however, many critics see it as outright heresy, an affront to the traditions of the sport. And therein lies one of the great blessings and burdens of the sport: Tradition."

—Lefty Kreh, with Chris Millard, *My Life Was THIS BIG and Other True Fishing Tales,* Skyhorse Publishing, 2008

202. The Importance of Casting Lefty's Way

"The old-fashioned 10 to 2 technique is adequate for that limited type of fishing [small-stream trout fishing]. . . . That technique does not work well when you are fishing for larger fish with larger flies on heavier lines over larger, windier bodies of water. As a result, most people who learn traditional casting technique while fishing for freshwater trout can't perform in other conditions."

—Lefty Kreh, with Chris Millard, *My Life Was THIS BIG and Other True Fishing Tales,* Skyhorse Publishing, 2008

203. Bluefish and Striper Migration Differences

Striped bass basically migrate north along the Atlantic coast in the spring, then south in the fall. Bluefish migrate from Atlantic depths offshore to preferred inshore areas in the spring, then fade back into the depths in the fall and early winter.

204. The Fall Striper Migration Run

The great fall striper migration run, a virtual living river of fish along the Atlantic coast, from Maine to North Carolina, takes place within a mile or so of shore. It varies with the run of the baitfish. Where the baitfish go, the stripers follow—from areas well offshore right up to the beach.

205. Misjudging Late-Fall Fishing

As a landlubber sensitive to temperature changes and the advent of winter, you might feel that those cold late-fall, early winter days have shut down the fishing. Perhaps it has, in fresh water, but the sea temperatures take time to drop, and fishing along the coast can be red-hot just when you're thinking the weather has turned too cold.

206. You'll Need a Gaff on the Jetties

"A longer gaff is important when fishing jetties, as it's often dangerous to scramble down to the water in order to land a big fish.

Jetty regulars carry longer gaffs strapped to their backs so they're not impeded when walking."

—Al Ristori, *The Complete Book of Surf Fishing*, Skyhorse Publishing, 2008

207. Sand Fleas: The Kind You Like

When you hear saltwater vets refer to sand fleas, they're not talking about insects that swarm and bite like regular "fleas." As Al Ristori tells us in his excellent *The Complete Book of Surf Fishing*, Skyhorse Publishing (2008), sand fleas are tiny crabs that scurry back and forth along the surfline and can be caught by hand. They make good bait for all kinds of saltwater denizens, particularly for that gourmet's delight, pompano.

208. Great Surf Fishing Starts Right Here

Al Ristori's *The Complete Book of Surf Fishing*, Skyhorse Publishing (2008), is the perfect starting point for getting into this rewarding and challenging fishing experience. From tackle to techniques, Ristori gives aspiring surf anglers all the solid, no-nonsense information they need to catch the fish that roam along the beaches. A legendary angler and writer from New Jersey, Ristori has fished many of the world's greatest beaches, and knows firsthand everything he writes about. When I look at his pictures of tarpon and snook in the surf beside the Parismina River in Costa Rica, I have to smile. It was there a leaping 90-pound tarpon knocked me overboard and broke my foot back in the 1970s. Al was there when it happened.

209. Spring Means Mackerel

They're sometimes called "little warriors," and the fishing fleets all along the Atlantic coast will be rigged and on the move for mackerel in March and early April. New Jersey, Long Island (especially Montauk), and points north usually get fantastic runs of little warriors that bring the first taste of spring to winter-weary anglers. Check your coastal listings and climb aboard. The action is fast, friendly, and rewarding.

210. Give Sea Trout Your Best Shot

Sea trout answer to many names, including spotted sea trout, speckled trout, and specks. In the mid-Atlantic saltwater regions, sea trout never achieve the box-office status of striped bass and bluefish, even though they are eagerly sought and caught at times. Head on down through the Carolinas and on around the coasts to the Gulf states and Texas, and you'll find where the sea trout really come into their own. Sea trout are outstanding on the table, one of the best. Best baits and lures include live shrimp worked over grassy flats in water 6 feet deep, over oyster bars, and at the mouths of tidal creeks.

CHAPTER 8

Wilderness Fishing

211. Canoe Trip Fishing: Base Camps Are Better

To each his own, but for my taste the fishing canoe trip where you're traveling every day, paddling hard to stay on a schedule, and moving from site to site isn't as much fun as setting up one or two base camps. I like to travel hard for perhaps a day and a half or two days, but then I want to be deep into good fishing country where I can set up a nice camp, stay for a spell, and catch my favorite fish—walleyes, lake trout, smallmouths, whatever. Obviously, there should be good fishing at this camp, and, hopefully, nearby waters that can be explored with day trips.

212. How to Shorten Canoe-Trip Portages

On your next canoe trip with a companion, when you have a lot of gear, consider cutting down on portage time by doing one and a half portages on those portages that usually require two trips. Your friend starts across with the canoe and one of the smaller packs. He takes this load all the way across the portage. You follow with the first load of packs. At the place where your best guesstimate says you've hit the halfway point, leave the packs and go back to the starting place for the others. Meanwhile your companion comes back along the portage to pick up the packs you left halfway. When you both reach the end of the portage, you will have made one and a half trips apiece over the entire portage length instead of two.

213. Those Very Special Mountain Brookies

"Mountain brookies are a special breed, although of the same spe-cies as the Eastern brook trout cousins of the rivers below. . . . I am advised by experts that the mountain relative of the large Labrador brookie lives but a brief four or five years. He is fragile, they say, and cannot withstand water temperatures above 75 degrees F."

—John Randolph, *Sports Afield*

214. Beaver Pond Brook Trout

"As I search for healthy ponds, I mark deep, dark water and cold inlet streams . . . I'll go alone when I go and come home alone and hide the path which has taken me out and in so no one else will cover my place . . . I'll talk a lot about these brookies in the high ponds, but I won't deal in revealing specifics. And other beaver pond anglers will understand why there's no invitation to come along, for they too have secret places and they too guard them closely. All know that one cannot share a beaver pond."

—John Randolph, *Sports Afield*

215. Finding Backcountry Hot spots

"In your research, don't overlook off-trail lakes that are close to roads. A lake that requires a 3-mile cross-country hike to reach may see fewer anglers than one 20 miles into the backcountry but right on a main trail."

—Rich Osthoff, *Fly Fishing the Rocky Mountain Backcountry*

216. Your Secret Backcountry Treasure

"Once you do find a good backcountry lake or stream, though, it's almost like owning private water. Just a handful of such spots can give you great angling for years to come."

—Rich Osthoff, *Fly Fishing the Rocky Mountain Backcountry*

217. Low Water Can Mean Canoe-Trip Nightmares

In low-water years of drought, or following such conditions, be aware that certain creeks and water courses that normally float your canoe will be muddy, boot-sucking bogs, extremely difficult to negotiate with your canoe and packs. What should have been an easy ride can turn into a nightmare in the sun, mud, sweat, and swarms of mosquitoes. On small watercourses where you were supposed to be paddling, not portaging, you'll be faced with the toughest conditions imaginable. Plan accordingly.

218. Canoe Trip's "Necessary" Extra

If you're going to paddle into a wilderness area and establish a base camp smack in the middle of good fishing, consider adding a tarp or fly to protect your cooking area or tent during periods of prolonged rain. In the spring or fall, especially, cold fronts can linger. There's not much worse than a soggy camp and gear.

219. Brook Trout Salvation

My friend Jim and I were young and strong, and we had come up to the Ontario wilderness to canoe a portion of the Drowning River, a tributary of the legendary Albany brook trout river. We took the train from Toronto to the town of Nakina, where our outfitter furnished us a canoe and packs and fly-in to a lake on the river. We were after brook trout, big brook trout, but what we found in massive quantities for our mid-July trip were mosquitoes and black flies. They nearly ate us alive, but we managed to portage the rapids, keep on paddling, and after three days and nights on the river, we spotted a tiny spring creek flowage into the river. The area was packed with big brookies, and we stayed there and caught them for two days before pushing on to the lake for our fly-out pickup. Had we not spotted that spring creek, the trip would have been a bust.

220. Brook Trout Salvation: Part Two

We were after brook trout on a canoe trip through Ontario's Algonquin Park, along the Petawawa River. Three days into the trip without a strike we found a section of the river where the water flowed from the lake through a creek-sized stream with long sets of small rapids and riffles. Brook trout charged our Mickey Finns and Edson Tigers from behind every rock it seemed. They were small fish, 10 inches or so, but they were wild trout, beautiful and tasty beyond words. We stayed there two days and the experience made our trip. Like the man said, "Size is not the measure."

221. The Smallmouth Transition

When I first began fishing the northern backcountry, I was not properly equipped with smallmouth lures. Being a good old boy, however, I had plenty of largemouth tackle, and I learned very quickly how to make it work for smallmouths: downsizing. When I went to much smaller lures and spinners, I began catching bronzebacks.

222. Curly-Tailed Grubs: The Backcountry Go-To Lure

Because they are so effective and in their soft-plastic state you can carry so many of them, curly-tailed and twister-tailed grubs rank as some of the deadliest lures you can carry into the backcountry. Two-inch sizes are the most popular, and they should be rigged with jig heads of 1/8 to ½ ounces. Whatever head you choose, always rig your grub with the hook pointing up and the tail pointing down. Popular colors are white, lime-green, yellow, and pearl.

223. Those Big Alaska Rainbows

If you go after the big rainbows out on the Alaska Peninsula, you'll find the fishing to be as varied as the terrain and weather. It is in late season, after the salmon runs have been progressing, that the rainbow fishing changes from traditional "fish the water" techniques to the great salmon-egg feast, with the rainbows gorging themselves on salmon eggs as they follow the runs of fish upstream. The eggs and patterns are all well-known to the guides, and the action can be furious. Sometimes the takes can be hard to spot, but, what the heck, with that many takes going on, you're bound to get your share of hookups. While fishing salmon eggs may not be as interesting as floating a dry fly or a mouse pattern over a rainbow hiding along a bank, the game is still appealing to any fly rodder.

224. Semi-Wild Smallmouth Fishing

I've been fortunate to do many canoe trips for wilderness smallmouths—particularly in the Boundary Waters-Quetico area and in Algonquin Park—and such trips have become personal favorites for dreaming and planning. In an attempt to mimic such fishing in areas closer to home where I live in the eastern United States, a number of years ago I began to do three-day float trips for smallmouths on the Upper Potomac river, particularly in the area from Paw Paw, West Virginia, down to Hancock, Maryland. Taking long weekends from Friday, we had two nights on the river and three days of floating and fishing. Canoes or jonboats will take you there, once you arrange your put-in and pull-out logistics. You won't feel like you're in the Quetico—more like in Deliverance country—but you'll find a nice slice of wilderness that's close to home.

225. Semi-Wild Smallmouth Fishing, Part Two

Bound for a pleasant couple of days floating a nice smallmouth stream like the Upper Potomac in West Virginia and Maryland, in mid- or late-summer you'll get your best results by wet-wading and carefully fishing the best-looking rapids, riffles, and sweeps of water. Don't race over and past them in your canoe or jonboat. It's time to get out and use your legs. This is fishing that cries out for light spinning tackle and flinging Mepps spinners across and down, working them into shadowy pockets and current seams where the fast water starts relaxing a bit. You might have a partner who insists on trying fly fishing for a time, and he's welcome to it. You'll make more casts, work more water, and catch more fish with light spinning tackle.

226. When The Plane Does Not Come

You may not need a bail-out bag (survival kit) in backcountry or canoe-trip fishing, but you do have to give some serious thought to the bag you'll need on the day (or days) when the plane does not come to fetch you for the trip home. If you fish enough in the backcountry, it will happen.

CHAPTER 9

Ice Fishing

227. The Truth About Ice Fishing

"Ice-fishing isn't so much a sport as it is a way of positively dealing with unfortunate reality. I mean, you can wake up in the morning depressed because it will be months yet before you can fly fish in real, liquid water, or you can leap out of bed thinking, 'Oh boy! It's the height of ice-fishing season.' Or if not, 'Oh boy,' then at least, 'Okay.'"

—John Gierach, *The View from Trout Lake,*
Simon & Schuster, 1988

228. Where the Fish Are

"Fish congregate under the ice, and do not spread out over the lake as in spring, summer, and fall. The deep holes are best, but these deep holes do not necessarily have to be in the middle of the lake."

—Charles J. Farmer, *Sports Afield*

229. Ice Fishing's Biggest Mistake

"The most common error I have seen in ice fishing is angling too far from shore. Think of the ice-covered lake as you would if you were covering it in a boat. Chances are you would not fish the middle of the lake, but rather you would cast to points, the drop-offs, and where streams enter the lake."

230. When Panfish Move Deeper

As the winter deepens and the action slows on your favorite areas along the banks for catching panfish—bluegills, yellow perch, pickerel— you may not have to chase all over the lake looking for them. First check out the deep water just adjacent to the areas where you caught panfish in summer and then at the start of winter's ice fishing.

231. Keeping Those Precious Smelt Alive

"Smelt are hard to get and hard to keep. They can't take sloshing around in bait buckets and will not be alive just when you need them most. Some anglers put baffles in their bait buckets to stop that from happening."

—Tom Hennessey

232. Modern Ice-Fishing Gear: The Key to Having Fun

"The snowmobile and power ice auger made ice fishing what it is today. In the days before these devices came along, ice fishing only called to the strongest and most hearty. All the equipment being used today—from power augers to rods, reels, and jigs— is amazing in what it can do to help you have fun days out on the ice, instead of drudgery and plain hard work. Check out the gear on the Internet, particularly at places like www.cabelas.com, www.basswpro.com, and www.gandermountain.com."

—Tom Hennessey

233. Check Those Traps Frequently

"Checking traps frequently can produce action with the bait that leads to strikes. Lifting the bait to check it gives it movement, action, attracting fish. Once attracted, they may start biting."

—Tom Hennessey

234. The Key to Taking Landlocks

"Landlock salmon move around the lake only a foot or two below the surface. Fish for them more shallow than other species."

—Tom Hennessey

235. Catching Lake Trout Through the Ice

"Best bait for lake trout (togue, to Maine folk) is a golden shiner or sucker, about 3 to 4 inches long. Make a cut just where the gills meet at the belly where there's an artery that will bleed. Find the bottom, then lift bait about a foot off it."

—Tom Hennessey

236. Setting Drag on Ice-Fishing Reels

"Basically, you want your ice-fishing reel to have little or no drag. Often when fish mouth the bait and feel tension, they will drop it. Fishing with no drag, you can set the hook after they've run a bit and taken the bait."

—Tom Hennessey

237. Best Ice-Fishing Rigs

"Use 6 to 8 feet of leader for deep fishing, less for the salmon, which move about only a foot or so below the ice. Use a swivel connected to line and use a No. 6 hook (or 4 sometimes). Use split-shot."

—Tom Hennessey

238. Using Smelt as Bait

"Smelt will swim around and around and twist line. They will come to the top if you don't have sinker."

—Tom Hennessey

239. Better Lure Action Under the Ice

Imagine an ice-fishing lure so effective it gives you the ability to "cast" under the ice. Sounds pretty good, don't you think? So do writers Ted Takasaki and Scott Richardson, who wrote on the tactics of ice-fishing guru Dave Genz in the article "Ice Spoonin' Walleyes" in the Articles section of the Lindy Tackle Web site, www.lindyfishingtackle.com. Genz especially likes first-ice walleyes when the oxygen levels and temps are more to their liking and they're more aggressive. He goes after them with Lindy's Rattlin' Flyer Spoon, with the look, flash, and sound that brings in walleyes, especially late in the afternoon when other lures are losing their effectiveness. The design of the Rattlin' Flyer, say Takasaki and Richardson, like its predecessor, the Flyer, allows the lure to have a gliding action when dropped into a hole, covering the water much like a cast. Genz uses a stiff-tip rod (limber tips won't give the lure action) and suggests on fishing the lure: "Don't lift it and let it pendulum back below the hole. Drag it. Twitch it as you drag it. Now, you're almost fishing like you would fish in summer." If you're a serious icefisher or a serious wannabe, check out all the details in this excellent article and many others at the Lindy site.

240. Early-Ice Walleye Spots to Set Up

Points that lead to drop-offs have always been known as prime walleye spots to put your ice auger to work on. Some experts tweak this idea with a further refinement: They choose the spots where the drop-off is the steepest, and is leading to the deepest part of the lake.

241. Working the Jig

The word "jigging" seems to be synonymous with ice fishing, and everybody seems to do it differently. Common knowledge, however, says to let the spoon or jig go all the way to the bottom, then lift it with a couple of cranks on your reel and keep it at that level as you make it flutter up and down.

242. Making Your Jig Even More Deadly

Bait fishermen with their tip-ups catch a lot of fish through the ice, but the method that's the most fun is jigging with a short rod. You can sweeten your jig by adding a minnow, hooked through the lips. The same rig is very effective in crappie fishing.

243. Better Way to Fish Jigging Spoons

"Jigging spoons usually have the hook on the fatter end and you tie your line to the thinner end. Reversing that will cause the lure to flutter more and keep it from dropping too fast."

—Larry Whiteley, OutdoorSite Library,
Bass Pro Shops, www.basspro.com

244. Don't Let Those Fish Freeze

"Don't let your fish freeze out on the ice unless you have a way of keeping them frozen. If they thaw out and you refreeze them when you get home, they will lose a lot of their flavor. "

—Larry Whiteley, OutdoorSite Library, Bass Pro Shops, www.basspro.com

245. Tackle for Hard-Water Bluegills

In an excellent article on the Bass Pro Shops' OutdoorSite Library, Jason Aki explains his tackle for consistently taking bluegills. "An ultralight to light jigging pole between 2 and 3 feet coupled to a micro spinning reel with line-holding capacity of 100 feet of 4-pound test . . . "

246. Lures and Rig for Hard-Water Bluegills

Continuing recommendations from Jason Aki in his article on jigging bluegills through the ice: "First off, line your rod with the lightest fishing line you feel confident in using, and then tie on a small spoon with the treble hook removed. Onto the bottom of the spoon tie a 10- or 12-inch leader of monofilament line and a small curved-shank hook. Onto the hook spear two to three wax worms or a dorsally hooked crappie minnow. The idea here is to have the spoon attract the bluegills' attention from a distance and the scent of the bait to get the fish to bite."

—Jason Aki, "Jigging Ice for Bluegill," OutdoorSite Library, Bass Pro Shops, www.basspro.com

247. Moving On to Better Things

"Small moves are tweaking your position on a piece of structure. They're 5- to 20-yard changes . . . Large moves are used to cover big distances. . . . Often it's better to move and try to find active fish than spend a lot of time with finicky fish. Sometimes, a few short moves will put you into biters, while some days are just tough bites."

—Tim Allard, "Ice Fishing a New Lake," OutdoorSite Library, Bass Pro Shops, www.basspro.com

248. Find the Fish with Sonar

"The sonar available to the modern ice angler is nothing short of amazing. In fact, many anglers don't even drill holes through the ice unless they first spot gamefish with their sonar. How is that possible? By simply pouring water on solid, clear ice and placing the transducer in the water, the unit can transmit and receive sound waves through the ice, allowing you to see the depth, weeds, and even fish."

—Gander Mountain article, www.gandermountain.com

249. The Yellow Perch Challenge

Yellow perch are a universal ice-fishing joy. They're great on the table, they usually roam the waters in schools, and they are widely distributed over North America's best ice-fishing destinations. While perch can be easy to find at times, they can also be difficult, zigging while you're zagging and vice versa. Before you can catch them, you have to find them—and it's not always that simple.

250. Yellow Perch Lures of an Expert

In an excellent article on the Bass Pro Shops Outdoor Library, angler Tim Allard says he divides his baits between "search" baits, which are relatively big jigging baits and "finesse" baits, for subtle jigging on holes where he knows there are fish. Allard tries to attract perch with relatively big jigging baits like Northland's Buckshot Spoon, Blue Fox's Rattle Flash Jig'n Spoons, Bay de Noc's Swedish Pimples, and Lindy's Rattlion Flyer. For subtle jigging he names ice jigs like Lindy Little Joe and Northland's Super Glo.